THE NEW FOLGER
SHAKESPEARE

Designed to make Shakespeare's great plays available to all readers, the New Folger Library edition of Shakespeare's plays provides accurate texts in modern spelling and punctuation, as well as scene-by-scene action summaries, full explanatory notes, many pictures clarifying Shakespeare's language, and notes recording all significant departures from the early printed versions. Each play is prefaced by a brief introduction, by a guide to reading Shakespeare's language, and by accounts of his life and theater. Each play is followed by an annotated list of further readings and by a "Modern Perspective" written by an expert on that particular play.

Barbara A. Mowat is Director of Research *emerita* at the Folger Shakespeare Library, Consulting Editor of *Shakespeare Quarterly*, and author of *The Dramaturgy of Shakespeare's Romances* and of essays on Shakespeare's plays and their editing.

Paul Werstine is Professor of English in the Graduate School and at King's University College at Western University. He is a general editor of the New Variorum Shakespeare and author of *Early Modern Playhouse Manuscripts and the Editing of Shakespeare*, as well as many papers and essays on the printing and editing of Shakespeare's plays.

Folger Shakespeare Library

The Folger Shakespeare Library in Washington, D.C., is a privately funded research library dedicated to Shakespeare and the civilization of early modern Europe. It was founded in 1932 by Henry Clay and Emily Jordan Folger, and incorporated as part of Amherst College in Amherst, Massachusetts, one of the nation's oldest liberal arts colleges, from which Henry Folger had graduated in 1879. In addition to its role as the world's preeminent Shakespeare collection and its emergence as a leading center for Renaissance studies, the Folger Shakespeare Library offers a wide array of cultural and educational programs and services for the general public.

EDITORS

BARBARA A. MOWAT
Director of Research emerita
Folger Shakespeare Library

PAUL WERSTINE
Professor of English
King's University College at Western University, Canada

FOLGER SHAKESPEARE LIBRARY

The Tragedy of

Macbeth

By
WILLIAM SHAKESPEARE

AN UPDATED EDITION

EDITED BY BARBARA A. MOWAT
AND PAUL WERSTINE

SIMON & SCHUSTER PAPERBACKS
NEW YORK LONDON TORONTO SYDNEY NEW DELHI

The sale of this book without its cover is unauthorized. If you purchased this book without a cover, you should be aware that it was reported to the publisher as "unsold and destroyed." Neither the author nor the publisher has received payment for the sale of this "stripped book."

Simon & Schuster Paperbacks
A Division of Simon & Schuster, Inc.
1230 Avenue of the Americas
New York, NY 10020

Copyright © 1992, 2013 by The Folger Shakespeare Library

All rights reserved, including the right to reproduce this book or portions thereof in any form whatsoever. For information, address Simon & Schuster Paperbacks Subsidiary Rights Department, 1230 Avenue of the Americas, New York, NY 10020.

This Simon & Schuster paperback edition October 2013

SIMON & SCHUSTER PAPERBACKS and colophon are registered trademarks of Simon & Schuster, Inc.

For information about special discounts for bulk purchases, please contact Simon & Schuster Special Sales at 1-866-506-1949 or business@simonandschuster.com

The Simon & Schuster Speakers Bureau can bring authors to your live event. For more information or to book an event contact the Simon & Schuster Speakers Bureau at 1-866-248-3049 or visit our website at www.simonspeakers.com.

Manufactured in the United States of America

30 29 28 27 26 25

ISBN: 978-1-4516-9472-7
ISBN: 978-1-4516-4454-8 (ebook)

From the Director of the Folger Shakespeare Library

It is hard to imagine a world without Shakespeare. Since their composition four hundred years ago, Shakespeare's plays and poems have traveled the globe, inviting those who see and read his works to make them their own.

Readers of the New Folger Editions are part of this ongoing process of "taking up Shakespeare," finding our own thoughts and feelings in language that strikes us as old or unusual and, for that very reason, new. We still struggle to keep up with a writer who could think a mile a minute, whose words paint pictures that shift like clouds. These expertly edited texts, presented here with accompanying explanatory notes and up-to-date critical essays, are distinctive because of what they do: they allow readers not simply to keep up, but to engage deeply with a writer whose works invite us to think, and think again.

These New Folger Editions of Shakespeare's plays are also special because of where they come from. The Folger Shakespeare Library in Washington, DC, where the Editions are produced, is the single greatest documentary source of Shakespeare's works. An unparalleled collection of early modern books, manuscripts, and artwork connected to Shakespeare, the Folger's holdings have been consulted extensively in the preparation of these texts. The Editions also reflect the expertise gained through the regular performance of Shakespeare's works in the Folger's Elizabethan Theater.

I want to express my deep thanks to editors Barbara Mowat and Paul Werstine for creating these indispensable editions of Shakespeare's works, which incorporate the best of textual scholarship with a richness of commentary that is both inspired and engaging. Readers who want to know more about Shakespeare and his plays can follow the paths these distinguished scholars have tread by visiting the Folger itself, where a range of physical and digital resources (available online) exist to supplement the material in these texts. I commend to you these words, and hope that they inspire.

Michael Witmore
Director, Folger Shakespeare Library

Contents

Editors' Preface	*ix*
Shakespeare's *Macbeth*	*xiii*
Reading Shakespeare's Language: *Macbeth*	*xvii*
Shakespeare's Life	*xxvii*
Shakespeare's Theater	*xxxvii*
The Publication of Shakespeare's Plays	*xlvii*
An Introduction to This Text	*li*
The Tragedy of Macbeth Text of the Play with Commentary	1
Longer Notes	*193*
Textual Notes	*197*
Macbeth: A Modern Perspective by Susan Snyder	*201*
Further Reading	*213*
Key to Famous Lines and Phrases	*247*

Editors' Preface

In recent years, ways of dealing with Shakespeare's texts and with the interpretation of his plays have been undergoing significant change. This edition, while retaining many of the features that have always made the Folger Shakespeare so attractive to the general reader, at the same time reflects these current ways of thinking about Shakespeare. For example, modern readers, actors, and teachers have become interested in the differences between, on the one hand, the early forms in which Shakespeare's plays were first published and, on the other hand, the forms in which editors through the centuries have presented them. In response to this interest, we have based our edition on what we consider the best early printed version of a particular play (explaining our rationale in a section called "An Introduction to This Text") and have marked our changes in the text—unobtrusively, we hope, but in such a way that the curious reader can be aware that a change has been made and can consult the "Textual Notes" to discover what appeared in the early printed version.

Current ways of looking at the plays are reflected in our brief introductions, in many of the commentary notes, in the annotated lists of "Further Reading," and especially in each play's "Modern Perspective," an essay written by an outstanding scholar who brings to the reader his or her fresh assessment of the play in the light of today's interests and concerns.

As in the Folger Library General Reader's Shakespeare, which The New Folger Library Shakespeare replaces, we include explanatory notes designed to help make Shakespeare's language clearer to a modern reader, and we place the notes on the page facing the text that they explain. We also follow the earlier edition in including illustrations—of objects, of clothing, of mythological figures—from books and manuscripts in the Folger Shakespeare Library collection. We provide fresh accounts of the life of Shakespeare, of the publishing of his plays, and of the theaters in which his plays were performed, as well as an introduction to the text itself. We also include a section called "Reading Shakespeare's Language," in which we try to help readers learn to "break the code" of Elizabethan poetic language.

For each section of each volume, we are indebted to a host of generous experts and fellow scholars. The "Reading Shakespeare's Language" sections, for example, could not have been written had not Arthur King, of Brigham Young University, and Randal Robinson, author of *Unlocking Shakespeare's Language*, led the way in untangling Shakespearean language puzzles and shared their insights and methodologies generously with us. "Shakespeare's Life" profited by the careful reading given it by S. Schoenbaum; "Shakespeare's Theater" was read and strengthened by Andrew Gurr, John Astington, and William Ingram; and "The Publication of Shakespeare's Plays" is indebted to the comments of Peter W. M. Blayney. We, as editors, take sole responsibility for any errors in our editions.

We are grateful to the authors of the "Modern Perspectives"; to Leeds Barroll and David Bevington for their generous encouragement; to the Huntington and Newberry Libraries for fellowship support; to King's University College for the grants it has provided to Paul Werstine; to the Social Sciences and Humanities Research Council of Canada, which has provided him with Research Time Stipends; to R. J. Shroyer of Western University for essential computer support;

Editors' Preface

and to the Folger Institute's Center for Shakespeare Studies for its fortuitous sponsorship of a workshop on "Shakespeare's Texts for Students and Teachers" (funded by the National Endowment for the Humanities and led by Richard Knowles of the University of Wisconsin), a workshop from which we learned an enormous amount about what is wanted by college and high-school teachers of Shakespeare today.

In preparing this preface for the publication of *Macbeth* in 1992, we wrote: Our biggest debt is to the Folger Shakespeare Library: to Werner Gundersheimer, Director of the Library, who has made possible our edition; to Jean Miller, the Library's Art Curator, who combed the Library holdings for illustrations, and to Julie Ainsworth, Head of the Photography Department, who carefully photographed them; to Peggy O'Brien, Director of Education, who gave us expert advice about the needs being expressed by Shakespeare teachers and students (and to Martha Christian and other "master teachers" who used our texts in manuscript in their classrooms); to the staff of the Academic Programs Division, especially Paul Menzer (who drafted "Further Reading" material), Mary Tonkinson, Lena Cowen Orlin, Molly Haws, and Jessica Hymowitz; and, finally, to the staff of the Library Reading Room, whose patience and support have been invaluable.

As we revise the play for publication in 2013, we add to the above our gratitude to Michael Witmore, Director of the Folger Shakespeare Library, who brings to our work a gratifying enthusiasm and vision; to Gail Kern Paster, Director of the Library from 2002 until July 2011, whose interest and support have been unfailing and whose scholarly expertise continues to be an invaluable resource; to Stephen Llano, our production editor at Simon & Schuster, whose expertise, attention to detail, and wisdom are essential to this project; to

Deborah Curren-Aquino, who provides extensive editorial and production support; to Alice Falk for her expert copyediting; to Michael Poston for unfailing computer support; and to the staff of the Library's Research Division, especially Christina Certo (whose help is crucial), David Schalkwyk (Director of Research), Mimi Godfrey, Kathleen Lynch, Carol Brobeck, Owen Williams, Sarah Werner, and Adrienne Schevchuk. Among the editions we consulted, we found A. R. Braunmuller's New Cambridge edition especially useful. Finally, we once again express our thanks to Jean Miller for the wonderful images she has unearthed, and to the ever-supportive staff of the Library Reading Room.

Barbara A. Mowat and Paul Werstine
2012

Shakespeare's *Macbeth*

In 1603, at about the middle of Shakespeare's career as a playwright, a new monarch ascended the throne of England. He was James VI of Scotland, who then also became James I of England. Immediately, Shakespeare's London was alive with an interest in things Scottish. Many Scots followed their king to London and attended the theaters there. Shakespeare's company, which became the King's Men under James's patronage, now sometimes staged their plays for the new monarch's entertainment, just as they had for Queen Elizabeth before him. It was probably within this context that Shakespeare turned to Raphael Holinshed's history of Scotland for material for a tragedy.

In Scottish history of the eleventh century, Shakespeare found a spectacle of violence—the slaughter of whole armies and of innocent families, the assassination of kings, the ambush of nobles by murderers, the brutal execution of rebels. He also came upon stories of witches and wizards providing advice to traitors. Such accounts could feed the new Scottish King James's belief in a connection between treason and witchcraft. James had already himself executed women as witches. Shakespeare's *Macbeth* supplied its audience with a sensational view of witches and supernatural apparitions and equally sensational accounts of bloody battles in which, for example, a rebel was "unseamed . . . from the nave [navel] to th' chops [jaws]."

It is possible, then, that in writing *Macbeth* Shakespeare was mainly intent upon appealing to the new interests in London brought about by James's kingship. What he created, though, is a play that has fascinated generations of readers and audiences that care

A Scottish king and his court.
From Raphael Holinshed, *The historie of Scotland* (1577).

little about Scottish history. In its depiction of a man who murders his king and kinsman in order to gain the crown, only to lose all that humans seem to need in order to be happy—sleep, nourishment, friends, love—*Macbeth* teases us with huge questions. Why do people do evil knowing that it is evil? Does Macbeth represent someone who murders because fate tempts him? because his wife pushes him into it? because he is overly ambitious? Having killed Duncan, why does Macbeth fall apart, unable to sleep, seeing ghosts, putting spies in everyone's home, killing his friends and innocent women and children? Why does the success of Macbeth and Lady Macbeth—prophesied by the witches, promising the couple power and riches and "peace to all their nights and days to come"—turn so quickly to ashes, destroying the Macbeths' relationship, their world, and, finally, both of them?

In earlier centuries, Macbeth's story was seen as a powerful study of a heroic individual who commits an evil act and pays an enormous price as his conscience—and the natural forces for good in the universe—destroy him. More recently, his story has been applied to nations that overreach themselves, his speeches of despair quoted to show that Shakespeare shared present-day feelings of alienation. Today, the line between Macbeth's evil and the supposed good of those who oppose him has been blurred, new attitudes about witches and witchcraft are being expressed, new questions raised about the ways that maleness and femaleness are portrayed in the play. Like so many of Shakespeare's plays, *Macbeth* speaks to each generation with a new voice.

After you have read the play, we invite you to read "*Macbeth:* A Modern Perspective" by the late Professor Susan Snyder of Swarthmore College.

Reading Shakespeare's Language: *Macbeth*

For many people today, reading Shakespeare's language can be a problem—but it is a problem that can be solved. Those who have studied Latin (or even French or German or Spanish) and those who are used to reading poetry will have little difficulty understanding the language of poetic drama. Others, however, need to develop the skills of untangling unusual sentence structures and of recognizing and understanding poetic compressions, omissions, and wordplay. And even those skilled in reading unusual sentence structures may have occasional trouble with Shakespeare's words. More than four hundred years of "static"— caused by changes in language and in life—intervene between his speaking and our hearing. Most of his vocabulary is still in use, but a few of his words are no longer used, and many of his words now have meanings quite different from those they had in the sixteenth and seventeenth centuries. In the theater, most of these difficulties are solved for us by actors who study the language and articulate it for us so that the essential meaning is heard—or, when combined with stage action, is at least *felt*. When we are reading on our own, we must do what each actor does: go over the lines (often with a dictionary close at hand) until the puzzles are solved and the lines yield up their poetry and the characters speak in words and phrases that are, suddenly, rewarding and wonderfully memorable.

Shakespeare's Words

As you begin to read the opening scenes of a Shakespeare play, you may notice occasional unfamiliar words. Some are unfamiliar simply because we no longer use them. In the opening scenes of *Macbeth*, for example, you will find the words *aroint thee* (begone), *coign* (corner), *anon* (immediately), *alarum* (a call to arms), *sewer* (butler), and *hautboy* (a very loud wind instrument designed for outdoor ceremonials, the forerunner of the orchestral oboe). Words of this kind are explained in notes to the text and will become familiar the more Shakespeare plays you read.

In *Macbeth*, as in all of Shakespeare's writing, more problematic are the words that are still in use but that now have different meanings. In the second scene of *Macbeth* we find the words *composition* (meaning "terms of peace") and *present* (meaning "immediate"); in the third scene, *choppy* is used where we would use "chapped" or "wrinkled," *addition* where we would use "title"; in the seventh scene, *receipt* is used to mean "container." Again, such words will be explained in the notes to the text, but they, too, will become familiar as you continue to read Shakespeare's language.

Some words are strange not because of the "static" introduced by changes in language over the past centuries but because these are words that Shakespeare is using to build a dramatic world that has its own space, time, and history. *Macbeth*, for example, builds, in its opening scenes, a location and a past history by references to "the Western Isles," to "thanes," "Sinel," "Glamis," and "Cawdor," to "kerns and gallowglasses," to "the Weïrd Sisters," to "Norweyan ranks," to "Inverness" and "Saint Colme's Inch." These "local" references build the Scotland that Macbeth and Lady

Macbeth inhabit and will become increasingly familiar to you as you get further into the play.

Shakespeare's Sentences

In an English sentence, meaning is quite dependent on the place given each word. "The dog bit the boy" and "The boy bit the dog" mean very different things, even though the individual words are the same. Because English places such importance on the positions of words in sentences, on the way words are arranged, unusual arrangements can puzzle a reader. Shakespeare frequently shifts his sentences away from "normal" English arrangements—often in order to create the rhythm he seeks, sometimes to use a line's poetic rhythm to emphasize a particular word, sometimes to give a character his or her own speech patterns or to allow the character to speak in a special way. When we attend a good performance of the play, the actors will have worked out the sentence structures and will articulate the sentences so that the meaning is clear. When reading the play, we need to do as the actor does: that is, when puzzled by a character's speech, check to see if the words are being presented in an unusual sequence.

Often Shakespeare rearranges subjects and verbs (i.e., instead of "He goes," we find "Goes he"). In the opening scenes of *Macbeth*, when Ross says (1.3.101–2) "As thick as tale / Came post with post," and when the witch says (1.3.24) "Shall he dwindle, peak, and pine," they are using constructions that place the subject and verb in unusual positions. The "normal" order would be "Post with post came as thick as tale" and "He shall dwindle...." Shakespeare also frequently places the object before the subject and verb (i.e., instead of "I hit him," we might find "Him I hit"). Banquo's statement to the Weïrd Sisters at 1.3.57–58, "My noble partner /

You greet with present grace and great prediction," is an example of such an inversion. (The normal order would be "You greet my noble partner with present grace and great prediction.") Lady Macbeth uses such an inverted structure in 1.7.73–74 when she says to Macbeth, "his two chamberlains / Will I with wine and wassail . . . convince" (where the "normal" structure would be "I will convince [i.e., overpower] his two chamberlains with wine and wassail").

In some plays Shakespeare makes systematic use of inversions (*Julius Caesar* is one such play). In *Macbeth*, he more often uses a different kind of unusual sentence structure, one that depends on the separation of words that would normally appear together. (Again, this is often done to create a particular rhythm or to stress a particular word.) Malcolm's "This is the sergeant / Who, like a good and hardy soldier, fought / 'Gainst my captivity" (1.2.4–6) separates the subject and verb ("who fought"); the Captain's "No sooner justice had, with valor armed, / Compelled these skipping kerns to trust their heels" (1.2.32–33) interrupts the two parts of the verb "had compelled" (at the same time that it inverts the subject and verb; the normal order would be "No sooner had justice compelled . . ."); a few lines later, the Captain's "the Norweyan lord, surveying vantage, / With furbished arms and new supplies of men, / Began a fresh assault" (1.2.34–36) separates the subject and verb ("lord began") with, first, a participial phrase and then a lengthy prepositional phrase. In order to create for yourself sentences that seem more like the English of everyday speech, you may wish to rearrange the words, putting together the word clusters and placing the remaining words in their more familiar order. You will usually find that the sentences will gain in clarity but will lose their rhythm or shift their emphases.

Locating and, if necessary, rearranging words that

Reading Shakespeare's Language   xxi

"belong together" is especially necessary in passages that separate subjects from verbs and verbs from objects by long delaying or expanding interruptions—a structure that is used frequently in *Macbeth*. For example, when the Captain, at 1.2.11–25, tells the story of Macbeth's fight against the rebel Macdonwald, he uses a series of such interrupted constructions:

> *The merciless Macdonwald*
> (Worthy to be a rebel, for to that
> The multiplying villainies of nature
> Do swarm upon him) from the Western Isles
> Of kerns and gallowglasses *is supplied*. . . .
> . . .
> But all's too weak;
> For *brave Macbeth* (well he deserves that name),
> Disdaining Fortune, with his brandished steel,
> Which smoked with bloody execution,
> Like Valor's minion, *carved out his passage* . . .

Here the interruptions provide details that catch the audience up in the Captain's story. The separation of the basic sentence elements "the merciless Macdonwald is supplied" forces the audience to attend to supporting details (of why he is worthy to be called a villain, of how he has been supplied with soldiers from the Western Isles) while waiting for the basic sentence elements to come together. A similar effect is created when "brave Macbeth carved out his passage" is interrupted by a clause commenting on the word "brave" ("well he deserves that name"), by a phrase that describes Macbeth's mood ("Disdaining Fortune"), and by two further phrases, one of them the complex "with his brandished steel / Which smoked with bloody execution," and one of them—"Like Valor's minion"—simple in structure but a richly rhetorical figure that makes Macbeth the chosen darling of Valor.

Occasionally, rather than separating basic sentence elements, Shakespeare simply holds them back, delaying them until much subordinate material has already been given. Lady Macbeth uses an inverted structure that provides this kind of delay when she says, at 1.6.22–24, "For those of old, / And the late dignities heaped up to them, / We rest your hermits" (where a "normally" constructed English sentence would have begun with the basic sentence elements "We rest your hermits"); Macbeth, in his famous soliloquy at 1.7.1–28, uses a delayed construction when he says (lines 2–7), "If th' assassination / Could trammel up the consequence and catch / With his surcease success, that but this blow / Might be the be-all and the end-all here, / But here, upon this bank and shoal of time, / We'd jump the life to come" (where the basic sentence elements "We'd jump the life to come" are delayed to the end of the very long sentence).

Shakespeare's sentences are sometimes complicated not because of unusual structures or interruptions or delays but because he omits words and parts of words that English sentences normally require. (In conversation, we, too, often omit words. We say, "Heard from him yet?" and our hearer supplies the missing "Have you." Frequent reading of Shakespeare—and of other poets—trains us to supply such missing words.) In *Macbeth,* Shakespeare uses omissions to great dramatic effect. At 1.3.105–8, Angus says to Macbeth, "We are sent / To give thee from our royal master thanks, / [We are sent] Only to herald thee into his sight, / Not [to] pay thee" (the omitted words, shown in brackets, add clarity but slow the speech). At 1.4.48–49, Duncan's cryptic "From hence to Inverness / And bind us further to you" would read, if the missing words were supplied, "Let us go from hence to Inverness, and may this visit bind us further to you." Lady Macbeth's soliloquy,

Reading Shakespeare's Language   xxiii

at 1.5.18–20, would read, with the omitted subjects and verbs in place, "Thou wouldst be great, / [Thou] Art not without ambition, but [thou art] without / The illness [that] should attend it." Later in the scene, at 1.5.51–54, she again omits words in saying, "Stop up th' access and passage to remorse, / [So] That no compunctious visitings of nature / [Will] Shake my fell purpose, nor keep peace between / Th' effect and it," and again at 1.7.80–82, where she asks Macbeth, "What [can]not [you and I] put upon / His spongy officers, who shall bear the guilt / Of our great quell?" In reading *Macbeth* one should stay alert for omitted words, since Shakespeare so often uses this device to build compression and speed in the language of this play.

Shakespearean Wordplay

Shakespeare plays with language so often and so variously that books are written on the topic. Here we will mention only two kinds of wordplay, puns and metaphors. A pun is a play on words that sound the same but have different meanings. In many plays (*Romeo and Juliet* is a good example) Shakespeare uses puns frequently; in *Macbeth* they are rarely found (except in such serious "punning" as Macbeth's "If it were done when 'tis done . . ." [1.7.1–2]). More such serious punning occurs in the exchange between Donalbain and Macbeth just after Duncan's murder. To Donalbain's request for information, "What is amiss?" (i.e., what's wrong?), Macbeth responds, "You are," punning on *amiss* as "damaged" (2.3.113–14). Perhaps the play's most famous (and the most shocking) pun is Lady Macbeth's "If he do bleed, / I'll gild the faces of the grooms withal, / For it must seem their guilt" (2.2.71–73), where she seems to be playing with the double meaning of *guilt/gilt*. Such wordplay is rare in *Macbeth*.

Metaphor, though, fills the play. A metaphor is a play on words in which one object or idea is expressed as if it were something else, something with which it is said to share common features. For instance, when Lady Macbeth says (1.5.28–29) "Hie thee hither, / That I may pour my spirits in thine ear," she is using metaphoric language: the words that she wants to say to Macbeth are compared to a liquid that can be poured in the ear. Metaphors are often used when the idea being conveyed is hard to express; through metaphor, the speaker is given language that helps to carry the idea or the feeling to his or her listener—and to the audience. Lady Macbeth uses metaphor to convey her contempt for Macbeth's cowardice (1.7.39–42): "Was the hope drunk / Wherein you dressed yourself? Hath it slept since? / And wakes it now, to look so green and pale / At what it did so freely?" And Macbeth expresses his own lack of valid motivation before the murder through a complex metaphor in which his "intent" is a horse and ambition is the knight preparing to ride the horse (1.7.25–27): "I have no spur / To prick the sides of my intent, but only / Vaulting ambition, which o'erleaps itself...."

Macbeth's Language

Each of Shakespeare's plays has its own characteristic language. The range of registers in *Macbeth*'s language, along with the denseness of its poetry, has attracted considerable critical attention. (See, e.g., "'What do you mean?': The Languages of *Macbeth*," in A. R. Braunmuller's New Cambridge edition of the play [updated edition, 2008, pages 43–55].) We would note here in

Reading Shakespeare's Language xxv

particular the deliberate imprecision of some of the play's words. Macbeth's lines (1.7.1–2) "If it were done when 'tis done, then 'twere well / It were done quickly" not only play with the imprecise verb "done" but also refer to some unnamed "it." In the next sentence, we learn that "it" is "th' assassination" (a word that Shakespeare invents for this play)—but the imprecision is characteristic of *Macbeth*'s language. We hear it again in Lady Macbeth's "Wouldst thou have that / Which thou esteem'st the ornament of life / And live a coward in thine own esteem . . . ? " (1.7.45–47), where "that which thou esteem'st the ornament of life" is, perhaps, the crown—or, perhaps, the kingship. The sense is clear, but the language seems deliberately vague, deliberately flowery, as if designed to cover over the serpent under it. Macbeth's prayer (3.2.52–56) that night use its "bloody and invisible hand" to "cancel and tear to pieces that great bond / Which keeps me pale" is a precisely relevant example of the kind of resonant imprecision that characterizes this play. (See longer note to 3.2.55, page 195.)

Implied Stage Action

Finally, in reading Shakespeare's plays we should always remember that what we are reading is a performance script. The dialogue is written to be spoken by actors who, at the same time, are moving, gesturing, picking up objects, weeping, shaking their fists. Some stage action is described in what are called "stage directions"; some is suggested within the dialogue itself. We must learn to be alert to such signals as we stage the play in our imaginations. When, in the third scene of *Macbeth*, Banquo says (1.3.44–47), "You seem to understand me / By each at once her choppy finger laying / Upon her skinny lips," the stage action is obvious. Again, his words to Macbeth (1.3.54–55), "Good sir, why do you start and seem to fear / Things that do sound so fair?," indicate that the actor playing Macbeth gestures in a fairly obvious way. It is less easy later in the scene to imagine exactly what is to take place just before Banquo says (1.3.82–83), "The earth hath bubbles, as the water has, / And these are of them. Whither are they vanished?" The director and the actors (and the reader, in imagination) must decide just how the witches melt "Like breath into the wind." The battle scenes in the fifth act of the play present a different kind of challenge to the reader's imagination, as Malcolm's army becomes a marching forest, and as Macbeth arms for battle, hears the ominous cry of women, kills young Siward, and then goes to meet his fate on the sword of Macduff. Learning to read the language of stage action repays one many times over when one reaches a crucial scene like that of the banquet and its appearing and disappearing ghost (3.4) or that of the final duel in 5.8—scenes in which implied stage action vitally affects our response to the play.

It is immensely rewarding to work carefully with Shakespeare's language so that the words, the sentences, the wordplay, and the implied stage action all become clear—as readers for the past four centuries have discovered. It may be more pleasurable to attend a good performance of a play—though not everyone has thought so. But the joy of being able to stage one of Shakespeare's plays in one's imagination, to return to passages that continue to yield further meanings (or further questions) the more one reads them—these are pleasures that, for many, rival (or at least augment) those of the performed text, and certainly make it worth considerable effort to "break the code" of Elizabethan poetic drama and let free the remarkable language that makes up a Shakespeare text.

Shakespeare's Life

Surviving documents that give us glimpses into the life of William Shakespeare show us a playwright, poet, and actor who grew up in the market town of Stratford-upon-Avon, spent his professional life in London, and returned to Stratford a wealthy landowner. He was born in April 1564, died in April 1616, and is buried inside the chancel of Holy Trinity Church in Stratford.

We wish we could know more about the life of the world's greatest dramatist. His plays and poems are testaments to his wide reading—especially to his knowledge of Virgil, Ovid, Plutarch, Holinshed's *Chronicles*, and the Bible—and to his mastery of the English language, but we can only speculate about his education. We know that the King's New School in Stratford-upon-Avon was considered excellent. The school was one of the English "grammar schools" established to educate young men, primarily in Latin grammar and literature. As in other schools of the time, students began their studies at the age of four or five in the attached "petty school," and there learned to read and write in English, studying primarily the catechism from the Book of Common Prayer. After two years in the petty school, students entered the lower form (grade) of the grammar school, where they began the serious study of Latin grammar and Latin texts that would occupy most of the remainder of their school days. (Several Latin texts that Shakespeare used repeatedly in writing his plays and poems were texts that schoolboys memorized and recited.) Latin comedies were introduced early in the lower form; in the upper form, which the boys entered at age ten or eleven, students wrote their own Latin orations and declamations, studied Latin

Title page of a 1573 Latin and Greek catechism for children. From Alexander Nowell, *Catechismus paruus pueris primum Latine* . . . (1573).

historians and rhetoricians, and began the study of Greek using the Greek New Testament. Since the records of the Stratford "grammar school" do not survive, we cannot prove that William Shakespeare attended the school; however, every indication (his father's position as an alderman and bailiff of Stratford, the playwright's own knowledge of the Latin classics, scenes in the plays that recall grammar-school experiences—for example, *The Merry Wives of Windsor*, 4.1) suggests that he did. We also lack generally accepted documentation about Shakespeare's life after his schooling ended and his professional life in London began. His marriage in 1582 (at age eighteen) to Anne Hathaway and the subsequent births of his daughter Susanna (1583) and the twins Judith and Hamnet (1585) are recorded, but how he supported himself and where he lived are not known. Nor do we know when and why he left Stratford for the London theatrical world, nor how he rose to be the important figure in that world that he had become by the early 1590s.

We do know that by 1592 he had achieved some prominence in London as both an actor and a playwright. In that year was published a book by the playwright Robert Greene attacking an actor who had the audacity to write blank-verse drama and who was "in his own conceit [i.e., opinion] the only Shake-scene in a country." Since Greene's attack includes a parody of a line from one of Shakespeare's early plays, there is little doubt that it is Shakespeare to whom he refers, a "Shake-scene" who had aroused Greene's fury by successfully competing with university-educated dramatists like Greene himself. It was in 1593 that Shakespeare became a published poet. In that year he published his long narrative poem *Venus and Adonis*; in 1594, he followed it with *The Rape of Lucrece*. Both poems were dedicated to the young earl of Southampton (Henry Wriothesley), who may have become Shakespeare's patron.

It seems no coincidence that Shakespeare wrote these narrative poems at a time when the theaters were closed because of the plague, a contagious epidemic disease that devastated the population of London. When the theaters reopened in 1594, Shakespeare apparently resumed his double career of actor and playwright and began his long (and seemingly profitable) service as an acting-company shareholder. Records for December of 1594 show him to be a leading member of the Lord Chamberlain's Men. It was this company of actors, later named the King's Men, for whom he would be a principal actor, dramatist, and shareholder for the rest of his career.

So far as we can tell, that career spanned about twenty years. In the 1590s, he wrote his plays on English history as well as several comedies and at least two tragedies (*Titus Andronicus* and *Romeo and Juliet*). These histories, comedies, and tragedies are the plays credited to him in 1598 in a work, *Palladis Tamia*, that in one chapter compares English writers with "Greek, Latin, and Italian Poets." There the author, Francis Meres, claims that Shakespeare is comparable to the Latin dramatists Seneca for tragedy and Plautus for comedy, and calls him "the most excellent in both kinds for the stage." He also names him "Mellifluous and honey-tongued Shakespeare": "I say," writes Meres, "that the Muses would speak with Shakespeare's fine filed phrase, if they would speak English." Since Meres also mentions Shakespeare's "sugared sonnets among his private friends," it is assumed that many of Shakespeare's sonnets (not published until 1609) were also written in the 1590s.

In 1599, Shakespeare's company built a theater for themselves across the river from London, naming it the Globe. The plays that are considered by many to be Shakespeare's major tragedies (*Hamlet, Othello, King Lear,* and *Macbeth*) were written while the company was resident in this theater, as were such comedies as *Twelfth Night* and *Measure for Measure*. Many of Shakespeare's plays were performed at court (both for Queen Elizabeth I and, after her death in 1603, for King James I), some were presented at the Inns of Court (the residences of London's legal societies), and some were doubtless performed in other towns, at the universities, and at great houses when the King's Men went on tour; otherwise, his plays from 1599 to 1608 were, so far as we know, performed only at the Globe. Between 1608 and 1612, Shakespeare wrote several plays—among them *The Winter's Tale* and *The Tempest*—presumably for the company's new indoor Blackfriars theater, though the plays seem to have been performed also at the Globe and at court. Surviving documents describe a performance of *The Winter's Tale* in 1611 at the Globe, for example, and performances of *The Tempest* in 1611 and 1613 at the royal palace of Whitehall.

Shakespeare wrote very little after 1612, the year in which he probably wrote *King Henry VIII*. (It was at a performance of *Henry VIII* in 1613 that the Globe caught fire and burned to the ground.) Sometime between 1610 and 1613 he seems to have returned to live in Stratford-upon-Avon, where he owned a large house and considerable property, and where his wife and his two daughters and their husbands lived. (His son Hamnet had died in 1596.) During his professional years in London, Shakespeare had presumably derived income from the acting company's profits as well as from his own career as an actor, from the sale of his play manuscripts to the acting company, and, after 1599, from his shares as an owner of the Globe. It was presumably that income, carefully invested in land

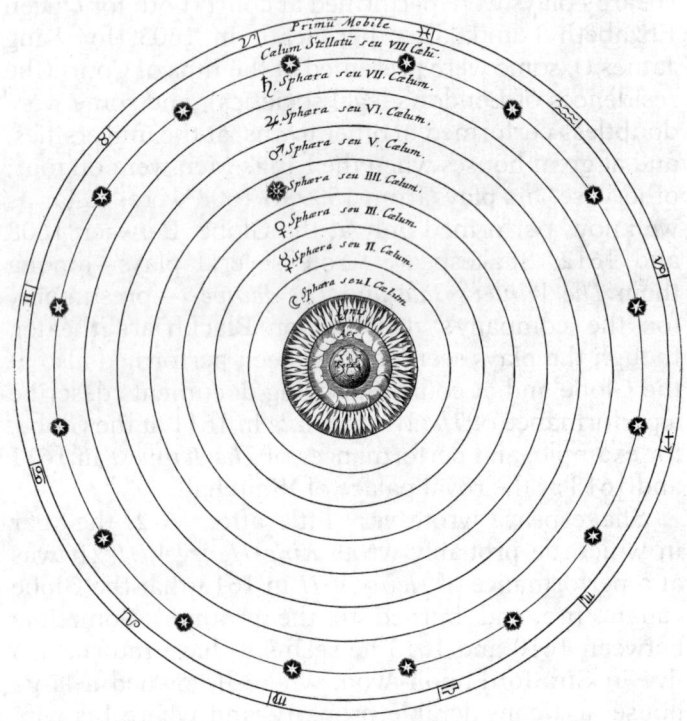

Ptolemaic universe.
From Marcus Manilius, *The sphere of* . . . (1675).

and other property, that made him the wealthy man that surviving documents show him to have become. It is also assumed that William Shakespeare's growing wealth and reputation played some part in inclining the Crown, in 1596, to grant John Shakespeare, William's father, the coat of arms that he had so long sought. William Shakespeare died in Stratford on April 23, 1616 (according to the epitaph carved under his bust in Holy Trinity Church) and was buried on April 25. Seven years after his death, his collected plays were published as *Mr. William Shakespeares Comedies, Histories, & Tragedies* (the work now known as the First Folio).

The years in which Shakespeare wrote were among the most exciting in English history. Intellectually, the discovery, translation, and printing of Greek and Roman classics were making available a set of works and worldviews that interacted complexly with Christian texts and beliefs. The result was a questioning, a vital intellectual ferment, that provided energy for the period's amazing dramatic and literary output and that fed directly into Shakespeare's plays. The Ghost in *Hamlet*, for example, is wonderfully complicated in part because he is a figure from Roman tragedy—the spirit of the dead returning to seek revenge—who at the same time inhabits a Christian hell (or purgatory); Hamlet's description of humankind reflects at one moment the Neoplatonic wonderment at mankind ("What a piece of work is a man!") and, at the next, the Christian disparagement of human sinners ("And yet, to me, what is this quintessence of dust?").

As intellectual horizons expanded, so also did geographical and cosmological horizons. New worlds—both North and South America—were explored, and in them were found human beings who lived and worshiped in ways radically different from those of Renaissance Europeans and Englishmen. The universe during these years also seemed to shift and expand. Copernicus had earlier theorized that the earth was not the center of the cosmos but revolved as a planet around the sun. Galileo's telescope, created in 1609, allowed scientists to see that Copernicus had been correct: the universe was not organized with the earth at the center, nor was it so nicely circumscribed as people had, until that time, thought. In terms of expanding horizons, the impact of these discoveries on people's beliefs—religious, scientific, and philosophical—cannot be overstated.

London, too, rapidly expanded and changed during the years (from the early 1590s to around 1610) that Shakespeare lived there. London—the center of England's government, its economy, its royal court, its overseas trade—was, during these years, becoming an exciting metropolis, drawing to it thousands of new citizens every year. Troubled by overcrowding, by poverty, by recurring epidemics of the plague, London was also a mecca for the wealthy and the aristocratic, and for those who sought advancement at court, or power in government or finance or trade. One hears in Shakespeare's plays the voices of London—the struggles for power, the fear of venereal disease, the language of buying and selling. One hears as well the voices of Stratford-upon-Avon—references to the nearby Forest of Arden, to sheepherding, to small-town gossip, to village fairs and markets. Part of the richness of Shakespeare's work is the influence felt there of the various worlds in which he lived: the world of metropolitan London, the world of small-town and rural England, the world of the theater, and the worlds of craftsmen and shepherds.

That Shakespeare inhabited such worlds we know from surviving London and Stratford documents, as well as from the evidence of the plays and poems themselves. From such records we can sketch the dramatist's life. We know from his works that he was a voracious reader. We know from legal and business documents that he was a multifaceted theater man who became a wealthy landowner. We know a bit about his family life and a fair amount about his legal and financial dealings. Most scholars today depend upon such evidence as they draw their picture of the world's greatest playwright. Such, however, has not always been the case. Until the late eighteenth century, the William Shakespeare who lived in most biographies was the creation of legend and tradition. This was the Shakespeare who was supposedly caught poaching deer at Charlecote, the estate of Sir Thomas Lucy close by Stratford; this was the Shakespeare who fled from Sir Thomas's vengeance and made his way in London by taking care of horses outside a playhouse; this was the Shakespeare who reportedly could barely read, but whose natural gifts were extraordinary, whose father was a butcher who allowed his gifted son sometimes to help in the butcher shop, where William supposedly killed calves "in a high style," making a speech for the occasion. It was this legendary William Shakespeare whose Falstaff (in *1* and *2 Henry IV*) so pleased Queen Elizabeth that she demanded a play about Falstaff in love, and demanded that it be written in fourteen days (hence the existence of *The Merry Wives of Windsor*). It was this legendary Shakespeare who reached the top of his acting career in the roles of the Ghost in *Hamlet* and old Adam in *As You Like It*—and who died of a fever contracted by drinking too hard at "a merry meeting" with the poets Michael Drayton and Ben Jonson. This legendary Shakespeare is a rambunctious, undisciplined man, as attractively "wild" as his plays were seen by earlier generations to be. Unfortunately, there is no trace of evidence to support these wonderful stories.

Perhaps in response to the disreputable Shakespeare of legend—or perhaps in response to the fragmentary and, for some, all-too-ordinary Shakespeare documented by surviving records—some people since the mid-nineteenth century have argued that William Shakespeare could not have written the plays that bear his name. These persons have put forward some dozen names as more likely authors, among them Queen Elizabeth, Sir Francis Bacon, Edward de Vere (earl of Oxford), and Christopher Marlowe. Such attempts to find what for these people is a more believable author of the plays is a tribute to the regard in which the plays are held. Unfortunately for their claims, the documents that exist that provide evidence for the facts of Shakespeare's life tie him inextricably to the body of plays and poems that bear his name. Unlikely as it seems to those who want the works to have been written by an aristocrat, a university graduate, or an "important" person, the plays and poems seem clearly to have been produced by a man from Stratford-upon-Avon with a very good "grammar-school" education and a life of experience in London and in the world of the London theater. How this particular man produced the works that dominate the cultures of much of the world almost four hundred years after his death is one of life's mysteries—and one that will continue to tease our imaginations as we continue to delight in his plays and poems.

Shakespeare's Theater

The actors of Shakespeare's time are known to have performed plays in a great variety of locations. They played at court (that is, in the great halls of such royal residences as Whitehall, Hampton Court, and Greenwich); they played in halls at the universities of Oxford and Cambridge, and at the Inns of Court (the residences in London of the legal societies); and they also played in the private houses of great lords and civic officials. Sometimes acting companies went on tour from London into the provinces, often (but not only) when outbreaks of bubonic plague in the capital forced the closing of theaters to reduce the possibility of contagion in crowded audiences. In the provinces the actors usually staged their plays in churches (until around 1600) or in guildhalls. While surviving records show only a handful of occasions when actors played at inns while on tour, London inns were important playing places up until the 1590s.

The building of theaters in London had begun only shortly before Shakespeare wrote his first plays in the 1590s. These theaters were of two kinds: outdoor or public playhouses that could accommodate large numbers of playgoers, and indoor or private theaters for much smaller audiences. What is usually regarded as the first London outdoor public playhouse was called simply the Theatre. James Burbage—the father of Richard Burbage, who was perhaps the most famous actor in Shakespeare's company—built it in 1576 in an area north of the city of London called Shoreditch. Among the more famous of the other public playhouses that capitalized on the new fashion were the Curtain and the Fortune (both also built north of the city), the Rose,

A stylized representation of the Globe theater.
From Claes Jansz Visscher, *Londinum florentissima Britanniae urbs* . . . [c. 1625].

the Swan, the Globe, and the Hope (all located on the Bankside, a region just across the Thames south of the city of London). All these playhouses had to be built outside the jurisdiction of the city of London because many civic officials were hostile to the performance of drama and repeatedly petitioned the royal council to abolish it.

The theaters erected on the Bankside (a region under the authority of the Church of England, whose head was the monarch) shared the neighborhood with houses of prostitution and with the Paris Garden, where the blood sports of bearbaiting and bullbaiting were carried on. There may have been no clear distinction between playhouses and buildings for such sports, for we know that the Hope was used for both plays and baiting and that Philip Henslowe, owner of the Rose and, later, partner in the ownership of the Fortune, was also a partner in a monopoly on baiting. All these forms of entertainment were easily accessible to Londoners by boat across the Thames or over London Bridge.

Evidently Shakespeare's company prospered on the Bankside. They moved there in 1599. Threatened by difficulties in renewing the lease on the land where their first theater (the Theatre) had been built, Shakespeare's company took advantage of the Christmas holiday in 1598 to dismantle the Theatre and transport its timbers across the Thames to the Bankside, where, in 1599, these timbers were used in the building of the Globe. The weather in late December 1598 is recorded as having been especially harsh. It was so cold that the Thames was "nigh [nearly] frozen," and there was heavy snow. Perhaps the weather aided Shakespeare's company in eluding their landlord, the snow hiding their activity and the freezing of the Thames allowing them to slide the timbers across to the Bankside without paying tolls for repeated trips over London Bridge.

Attractive as this narrative is, it remains just as likely that the heavy snow hampered transport of the timbers in wagons through the London streets to the river. It also must be remembered that the Thames was, according to report, only "nigh frozen," and therefore did not necessarily provide solid footing. Whatever the precise circumstances of this fascinating event in English theater history, Shakespeare's company was able to begin playing at their new Globe theater on the Bankside in 1599. After this theater burned down in 1613 during the staging of Shakespeare's *Henry VIII* (its thatch roof was set alight by cannon fire called for in performance), Shakespeare's company immediately rebuilt on the same location. The second Globe seems to have been a grander structure than its predecessor. It remained in use until the beginning of the English Civil War in 1642, when Parliament officially closed the theaters. Soon thereafter it was pulled down.

The public theaters of Shakespeare's time were very different buildings from our theaters today. First of all, they were open-air playhouses. As recent excavations of the Rose and the Globe confirm, some were polygonal or roughly circular in shape; the Fortune, however, was square. The most recent estimates of their size put the diameter of these buildings at 72 feet (the Rose) to 100 feet (the Globe), but we know that they held vast audiences of two or three thousand, who must have been squeezed together quite tightly. Some of these spectators paid extra to sit or stand in the two or three levels of roofed galleries that extended, on the upper levels, all the way around the theater and surrounded an open space. In this space were the stage and, perhaps, the tiring house (what we would call dressing rooms), as well as the so-called yard. In the yard stood the spectators who chose to pay less, the ones whom Hamlet contemptuously called "groundlings." For a roof they had only the sky, and so they were exposed to all kinds of weather. They stood on a floor that was sometimes made of mortar and sometimes of ash mixed with the shells of hazelnuts, which, it has recently been discovered, were standard flooring material in the period. Unlike the yard, the stage itself was covered by a roof. Its ceiling, called "the heavens," is thought to have been elaborately painted to depict the sun, moon, stars, and planets. The exact size of the stage remains hard to determine. We have a single sketch of part of the interior of the Swan. A Dutchman named Johannes de Witt visited this theater around 1596 and sent a sketch of it back to his friend, Arend van Buchel. Because van Buchel found de Witt's letter and sketch of interest, he copied both into a book. It is van Buchel's copy, adapted, it seems, to the shape and size of the page in his book, that survives. In this sketch, the stage appears to be a large rectangular platform that thrusts far out into the yard, perhaps even as far as the center of the circle formed by the surrounding galleries. This drawing, combined with the specifications for the size of the stage in the building contract for the Fortune, has led scholars to conjecture that the stage on which Shakespeare's plays were performed must have measured approximately 43 feet in width and 27 feet in depth, a vast acting area. But the digging up of a large part of the Rose by late-twentieth-century archaeologists has provided evidence of a quite different stage design. The Rose stage was a platform tapered at the corners and much shallower than what seems to be depicted in the van Buchel sketch. Indeed, its measurements seem to be about 37.5 feet across at its widest point and only 15.5 feet deep. Because the surviving indications of stage size and design differ from each other so much, it is possible that the stages in other theaters, like the Theatre, the Curtain, and the Globe (the outdoor playhouses where we know that Shakespeare's plays were performed), were different from those at both the Swan and the Rose.

After about 1608 Shakespeare's plays were staged not only at the Globe but also at an indoor or private playhouse in Blackfriars. This theater had been constructed in 1596 by James Burbage in an upper hall of a former Dominican priory or monastic house. Although Henry VIII had dissolved all English monasteries in the 1530s (shortly after he had founded the Church of England), the area remained under church, rather than hostile civic, control. The hall that Burbage had purchased and renovated was a large one in which Parliament had once met. In the private theater that he constructed, the stage, lit by candles, was built across the narrow end of the hall, with boxes flanking it. The rest of the hall offered seating room only. Because there was no provision for standing room, the largest audience it could hold was less than a thousand, or about a quarter of what the Globe could accommodate. Admission to Blackfriars was correspondingly more expensive. Instead of a penny to stand in the yard at the Globe, it cost a minimum of sixpence to get into Blackfriars. The best seats at the Globe (in the Lords' Room in the gallery above and behind the stage) cost sixpence; but the boxes flanking the stage at Blackfriars were half a crown, or five times sixpence. Some spectators who were particularly interested in displaying themselves paid even more to sit on stools on the Blackfriars stage.

Whether in the outdoor or indoor playhouses, the stages of Shakespeare's time were different from ours. They were not separated from the audience by the dropping of a curtain between acts and scenes. Therefore the playwrights of the time had to find other ways of signaling to the audience that one scene (to be imagined as occurring in one location at a given time) had ended and the next (to be imagined at perhaps a different location at a later time) had begun. The customary way used by Shakespeare and many of his contemporaries was to have everyone on stage exit at the end of one scene and have one or more different characters enter to begin the next. In a few cases, where characters remain onstage from one scene to another, the dialogue or stage action makes the change of location clear, and the characters are generally to be imagined as having moved from one place to another. For example, in *Romeo and Juliet*, Romeo and his friends remain onstage in Act 1 from scene 4 to scene 5, but they are represented as having moved between scenes from the street that leads to Capulet's house into Capulet's house itself. The new location is signaled in part by the appearance onstage of Capulet's servingmen carrying napkins, something they would not take into the streets. Playwrights had to be quite resourceful in the use of hand properties, like the napkin, or in the use of dialogue to specify where the action was taking place in their plays because, in contrast to most of today's theaters, the playhouses of Shakespeare's time did not fill the stage with scenery to make the setting precise. A consequence of this difference was that the playwrights of Shakespeare's time did not have to specify exactly where the action of their plays was set when they did not choose to do so, and much of the action of their plays is tied to no specific place.

Usually Shakespeare's stage is referred to as a "bare stage," to distinguish it from the stages of the last two or three centuries with their elaborate sets. But the stage in Shakespeare's time was not completely bare. Philip Henslowe, owner of the Rose, lists in his inventory of stage properties a rock, three tombs, and two mossy banks. Stage directions in plays of the time also call for such things as thrones (or "states"), banquets (presumably tables with plaster replicas of food on them), and beds and tombs to be pushed onto the stage. Thus the stage often held more than the actors. The actors did not limit their performing to the stage alone. Occasionally they went beneath the stage, as the Ghost appears to do in the first act of *Hamlet*. From there they could emerge onto the stage through a trapdoor. They could retire behind the hangings across the back of the stage, as, for example, the actor playing Polonius does when he hides behind the arras. Sometimes the hangings could be drawn back during a performance to "discover" one or more actors behind them. When performance required that an actor appear "above," as when Juliet is imagined to stand at the window of her chamber in the famous and misnamed "balcony scene," then the actor probably climbed the stairs to the gallery over the back of the stage and temporarily shared it with some of the spectators. The stage was also provided with ropes and winches so that actors could descend from, and reascend to, the "heavens."

Perhaps the greatest difference between dramatic performances in Shakespeare's time and ours was that in Shakespeare's England the roles of women were played by boys. (Some of these boys grew up to take male roles in their maturity.) There were no women in the acting companies. It had not always been so in the history of the English stage. There are records of women on English stages in the thirteenth and fourteenth centuries, two hundred years before Shakespeare's plays were performed. After the accession of James I in 1603, the queen of England and her ladies took part in entertainments at court called masques, and with the reopening of the theaters in 1660 at the restoration of Charles II, women again took their place on the public stage.

Shakespeare's Theater

The chief competitors of such acting companies as the one to which Shakespeare belonged and for which he wrote were companies of exclusively boy actors. The competition was most intense in the early 1600s. There were then two principal children's companies: the Children of Paul's (the choirboys from St. Paul's Cathedral, whose private playhouse was near the cathedral); and the Children of the Chapel Royal (the choirboys from the monarch's private chapel, who performed at the Blackfriars theater built by Burbage in 1596). In *Hamlet* Shakespeare writes of "an aerie [nest] of children, little eyases [hawks], that cry out on the top of question and are most tyrannically clapped for 't. These are now the fashion and . . . berattle the common stages [attack the public theaters]." In the long run, the adult actors prevailed. The Children of Paul's dissolved around 1606. By about 1608 the Children of the Chapel Royal had been forced to stop playing at the Blackfriars theater, which was then taken over by the King's Men, Shakespeare's own troupe.

Acting companies and theaters of Shakespeare's time seem to have been organized in various ways. For example, with the building of the Globe, Shakespeare's company apparently managed itself, with the principal actors, Shakespeare among them, having the status of "sharers" and the right to a share in the takings, as well as the responsibility for a part of the expenses. Five of the sharers, including Shakespeare, owned the Globe. As actor, as sharer in an acting company and in ownership of theaters, and as playwright, Shakespeare was about as involved in the theatrical industry as one could imagine. Although Shakespeare and his fellows prospered, their status under the law was conditional upon the protection of powerful patrons. "Common players"—those who did not have patrons or masters—were classed in the language of the law with "vagabonds and sturdy beggars." So the actors had to secure for themselves the official rank of servants of patrons. Among the patrons under whose protection Shakespeare's company worked were the lord chamberlain and, after the accession of King James in 1603, the king himself.

In the early 1990s we seemed on the verge of learning a great deal more about the theaters in which Shakespeare and his contemporaries performed—or, at least, opening up new questions about them. At that time about 70 percent of the Rose had been excavated, as had about 10 percent of the second Globe, the one built in 1614. It was then hoped that more would become available for study. However, excavation was halted at that point, and while it is not known if or when it will resume at these sites, archaeological discoveries in Shoreditch in 2008 in the vicinity of the Theatre may yield new information about the playhouses of Shakespeare's London.

The Publication of Shakespeare's Plays

Eighteen of Shakespeare's plays found their way into print during the playwright's lifetime, but there is nothing to suggest that he took any interest in their publication. These eighteen appeared separately in editions in quarto or, in the case of *Henry VI, Part 3*, octavo format. The quarto pages are not much larger than a modern mass-market paperback book, and the octavo pages are even smaller; these little books were sold unbound for a few pence. The earliest of the quartos that still survive were printed in 1594, the year that both *Titus Andronicus* and a version of the play now called *Henry VI, Part 2* became available. While almost every one of these early quartos displays on its title page the name of the acting company that performed the play, only about half provide the name of the playwright, Shakespeare. The first quarto edition to bear the name Shakespeare on its title page is *Love's Labor's Lost* of 1598. A few of the quartos were popular with the book-buying public of Shakespeare's lifetime; for example, quarto *Richard II* went through five editions between 1597 and 1615. But most of the quartos were far from best sellers; *Love's Labor's Lost* (1598), for instance, was not reprinted in quarto until 1631. After Shakespeare's death, two more of his plays appeared in quarto format: *Othello* in 1622 and *The Two Noble Kinsmen*, coauthored with John Fletcher, in 1634.

In 1623, seven years after Shakespeare's death, *Mr. William Shakespeares Comedies, Histories, & Tragedies* was published. This printing offered readers in a single book thirty-six of the thirty-eight plays now thought to have been written by Shakespeare, including eighteen that had never been printed before. And it offered them in a style that was then reserved for serious literature and scholarship. The plays were arranged in double columns on pages nearly a foot high. This large page size is called "folio," as opposed to the smaller "quarto," and the 1623 volume is usually called the Shakespeare First Folio. It is reputed to have sold for the lordly price of a pound. (One copy at the Folger Shakespeare Library is marked fifteen shillings—that is, three-quarters of a pound.)

In a preface to the First Folio entitled "To the great Variety of Readers," two of Shakespeare's former fellow actors in the King's Men, John Heminge and Henry Condell, wrote that they themselves had collected their dead companion's plays. They suggested that they had seen his own papers: "we have scarce received from him a blot in his papers." The title page of the Folio declared that the plays within it had been printed "according to the True Original Copies." Comparing the Folio to the quartos, Heminge and Condell disparaged the quartos, advising their readers that "before you were abused with divers stolen and surreptitious copies, maimed, and deformed by the frauds and stealths of injurious impostors." Many Shakespeareans of the eighteenth and nineteenth centuries believed Heminge and Condell and regarded the Folio plays as superior to anything in the quartos.

Once we begin to examine the Folio plays in detail, it becomes less easy to take at face value the word of Heminge and Condell about the superiority of the Folio texts. For example, of the first nine plays in the Folio (one-quarter of the entire collection), four were essentially reprinted from earlier quarto printings that Heminge and Condell had disparaged, and four have now been identified as printed from copies written in

The Publication of Shakespeare's Plays   xlix

the hand of a professional scribe of the 1620s named Ralph Crane; the ninth, *The Comedy of Errors*, was apparently also printed from a manuscript, but one whose origin cannot be readily identified. Evidently, then, eight of the first nine plays in the First Folio were not printed, in spite of what the Folio title page announces, "according to the True Original Copies," or Shakespeare's own papers, and the source of the ninth is unknown. Since today's editors have been forced to treat Heminge and Condell's pronouncements with skepticism, they must choose whether to base their own editions upon quartos or the Folio on grounds other than Heminge and Condell's story of where the quarto and Folio versions originated.

Editors have often fashioned their own narratives to explain what lies behind the quartos and Folio. They have said that Heminge and Condell meant to criticize only a few of the early quartos, the ones that offer much shorter and sometimes quite different, often garbled, versions of plays. Among the examples of these are the 1600 quarto of *Henry V* (the Folio offers a much fuller version) or the 1603 *Hamlet* quarto. (In 1604 a different, much longer form of the play got into print as a quarto.) Early twentieth-century editors speculated that these questionable texts were produced when someone in the audience took notes from the plays' dialogue during performances and then employed "hack poets" to fill out the notes. The poor results were then sold to a publisher and presented in print as Shakespeare's plays. More recently this story has given way to another in which the shorter versions are said to be re-creations from memory of Shakespeare's plays by actors who wanted to stage them in the provinces but lacked manuscript copies. Most of the quartos offer much better texts than these so-called bad quartos. Indeed, in most of the quartos we find texts that are at least equal to or better than what is printed in the Folio. Many Shakespeare enthusiasts persuaded themselves that most of the quartos were set into type directly from Shakespeare's own papers, although there is nothing on which to base this conclusion except the desire for it to be true. Thus speculation continues about how the Shakespeare plays got to be printed. All that we have are the printed texts.

The book collector who was most successful in bringing together copies of the quartos and the First Folio was Henry Clay Folger, founder of the Folger Shakespeare Library in Washington, D.C. While it is estimated that there survive around the world only about 230 copies of the First Folio, Mr. Folger was able to acquire more than seventy-five copies, as well as a large number of fragments, for the library that bears his name. He also amassed a substantial number of quartos. For example, only fourteen copies of the First Quarto of *Love's Labor's Lost* are known to exist, and three are at the Folger Shakespeare Library. As a consequence of Mr. Folger's labors, scholars visiting the Folger Shakespeare Library have been able to learn a great deal about sixteenth- and seventeenth-century printing and, particularly, about the printing of Shakespeare's plays. And Mr. Folger did not stop at the First Folio, but collected many copies of later editions of Shakespeare, beginning with the Second Folio (1632), the Third (1663–64), and the Fourth (1685). Each of these later folios was based on its immediate predecessor and was edited anonymously. The first editor of Shakespeare whose name we know was Nicholas Rowe, whose first edition came out in 1709. Mr. Folger collected this edition and many, many more by Rowe's successors, and the collecting continues.

An Introduction to This Text

Macbeth was first printed in the 1623 collection of Shakespeare's plays now known as the First Folio. (Since the nineteenth century there have been scholars and editors who believe that parts of *Macbeth* as it appears in the Folio were written not by Shakespeare but by Thomas Middleton. Such scholars have offered to identify precisely Middleton's contributions to the play, but their attributions to him remain the subject of fierce controversy. See our scene heading for 3.5 and our commentary on 4.1.38 SD–43 and 141–48 for notes on some such passages.) The present edition of the play is based directly upon the 1623 printing.* For the convenience of the reader, we have modernized the punctuation and the spelling of the First Folio. Sometimes we go so far as to modernize certain old forms of words; for example, when *a* means "he," we change it to *he*; we change *mo* to *more* and *ye* to *you*. But it is not our practice in editing any of the plays to modernize forms of words that sound distinctly different from modern forms. For example, when the early printed text reads *sith* or *apricocks* or *porpentine*, we have not modernized to *since, apricots, porcupine*. When the forms *an, and,* or *and if* appear instead of the modern form *if,* we have reduced *and* to *an* but have not changed any of these forms to their modern equivalent, *if*. We also modernize and, where necessary, correct passages in foreign languages, unless an error in the early printed text can be reasonably explained as a joke.

---

*We have also consulted the computerized text of the First Folio provided by the Text Archive of the Oxford University Computing Centre, to which we are grateful.

li

Whenever we change the wording of the First Folio or add anything to its stage directions, we mark the change by enclosing it in superior half-brackets (⌜ ⌝). We want our readers to be immediately aware when we have intervened. (Only when we correct an obvious typographical error in the First Folio does the change not get marked.) Whenever we change the First Folio's wording or change its punctuation so that the meaning changes, we list the change in the textual notes at the back of the book, even if all we have done is fix an obvious error.

We correct or regularize a number of the proper names, as is the usual practice in editions of the play. For example, the Folio's occasional spelling "Dunsmane" is altered to "Dunsinane," the Folio's more usual spelling, and the various Folio spellings of Birnam Wood—"Byrnam," "Byrnan," "Birnan," "Byrnane," and "Birnane"—are all spelled "Birnam" in this edition. Since no scholars believe that the Folio *Macbeth* was printed directly from Shakespeare's own papers, it would be difficult to identify the Folio's spellings of names as Shakespeare's preferences.

This edition differs from many earlier ones in its efforts to aid the reader in imagining the play as a performance, rather than as a series of historical events. Thus stage directions are written with reference to the stage. For example, at 2.3.20, instead of providing a stage direction that says "The Porter opens the gate," as many editions do, this edition has "The Porter opens the door." There may have been doors on Shakespeare's stages for the Porter to open, but almost certainly there were no gates.

Whenever it is reasonably certain, in our view, that a speech is accompanied by a particular action, we provide a stage direction describing the action. (Occasional exceptions to this rule occur when the action is

An Introduction to This Text liii

so obvious that to add a stage direction would insult the reader.) Stage directions for the entrance of characters in mid-scene are, with rare exceptions, placed so that they immediately precede the characters' participation in the scene, even though these entrances may appear somewhat earlier in the early printed texts. Whenever we move a stage direction, we record this change in the textual notes. Latin stage directions (e.g., *Exeunt*) are translated into English (e.g., *They exit*).

We expand the often severely abbreviated forms of names used as speech headings in early printed texts into the full names of the characters. We also regularize the speakers' names in speech headings, using only a single designation for each character, even though the early printed texts sometimes use a variety of designations. Variations in the speech headings of the early printed texts are recorded in the textual notes.

In the present edition, as well, we mark with a dash any change of address within a speech, unless a stage direction intervenes. When the *-ed* ending of a word is to be pronounced, we mark it with an accent. Like editors for the last two centuries, we print metrically linked lines in the following way:

MACBETH
    We will speak further.
LADY MACBETH   Only look up clear.

However, when there are a number of short verse-lines that can be linked in more than one way, we do not, with rare exceptions, indent any of them.

The Explanatory Notes

The notes that appear on the pages facing the text are designed to provide readers with the help that they may need to enjoy the play. Whenever the meaning of a word in the text is not readily accessible in a good contemporary dictionary, we offer the meaning in a note. Sometimes we provide a note even when the relevant meaning is to be found in the dictionary but when the word has acquired since Shakespeare's time other potentially confusing meanings. In our notes, we try to offer modern synonyms for Shakespeare's words. We also try to indicate to the reader the connection between the word in the play and the modern synonym. For example, Shakespeare sometimes uses the word *head* to mean "source," but, for modern readers, there may be no connection evident between these two words. We provide the connection by explaining Shakespeare's usage as follows: "**head:** fountainhead, source." On some occasions, a whole phrase or clause needs explanation. Then, if space allows, we rephrase in our own words the difficult passage, and add at the end synonyms for individual words in the passage. When scholars have been unable to determine the meaning of a word or phrase, we acknowledge the uncertainty. Biblical quotations are from the Geneva Bible (1560), with spelling modernized.

The Tragedy of
MACBETH

Characters in the Play

Three Witches, the Weïrd Sisters

DUNCAN, king of Scotland
MALCOLM, his elder son
DONALBAIN, Duncan's younger son

MACBETH, thane of Glamis
LADY MACBETH
SEYTON, attendant to Macbeth
Three Murderers in Macbeth's service
A Doctor ⎱ *both attending upon Lady Macbeth*
A Gentlewoman ⎰
A Porter

BANQUO, commander, with Macbeth, of Duncan's army
FLEANCE, his son

MACDUFF, a Scottish noble
LADY MACDUFF
Their son

LENNOX ⎫
ROSS ⎪
ANGUS ⎬ *Scottish nobles*
MENTEITH ⎪
CAITHNESS ⎭

SIWARD, commander of the English forces
YOUNG SIWARD, Siward's son

A Captain in Duncan's army
An Old Man
A Doctor at the English court

3

HECATE

Apparitions: an Armed Head, a Bloody Child, a Crowned Child, and eight nonspeaking kings

Three Messengers, Three Servants, a Lord, a Soldier

Attendants, a Sewer, Servants, Lords, Thanes, Soldiers (all nonspeaking)

The Tragedy of
MACBETH

ACT 1

1.1 Three witches plan to meet Macbeth.

---

3. **When the hurly-burly's done: When the** turmoil is over; after the battle
5. **ere:** before
9. **Graymalkin:** the name of the first witch's "familiar" (an attendant spirit serving her in the form of a cat)
10. **Paddock:** a toad, the familiar of the second witch (See picture, below.)
11. **Anon:** immediately (perhaps, the response of the third witch to her familiar)
13. **filthy:** murky, thick

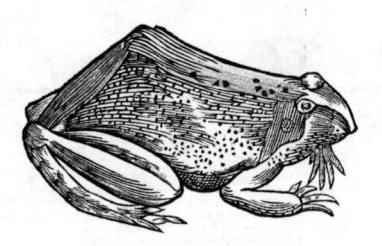

A toad. (1.1.10; 4.1.6)
From Edward Topsell, *The historie of serpents* . . . (1608).

ACT 1

Scene 1

Thunder and lightning. Enter three Witches.

FIRST WITCH
  When shall we three meet again?
  In thunder, lightning, or in rain?
SECOND WITCH
  When the hurly-burly's done,   *battle*
  When the battle's lost and won.
THIRD WITCH
  That will be ere the set of sun.   5
FIRST WITCH
  Where the place?
SECOND WITCH   Upon the heath.
THIRD WITCH
  There to meet with Macbeth.
FIRST WITCH   I come, Graymalkin.
⌜SECOND WITCH⌝   Paddock calls.   10
⌜THIRD WITCH⌝   Anon.
ALL   *things aren't as they seem*
  Fair is foul, and foul is fair;
  Hover through the fog and filthy air.
                              They exit.

1.2 Duncan, king of Scotland, hears an account of the success in battle of his noblemen Macbeth and Banquo. Duncan orders the execution of the rebel thane of Cawdor and sends messengers to announce to Macbeth that he has been given Cawdor's title.

---

0 SD. **Alarum:** a trumpet "call to arms"; **within:** offstage

4. **sergeant:** soldier, officer (also called *Captain* in the Folio stage directions and speech prefixes)

7. **broil:** i.e., battle

10. **spent:** exhausted

11. **choke their art:** prevent each other from using their skill (in swimming)   **art:** skill

12. **to that: to** make him **that** (i.e., **a rebel**)

13. **villainies:** shameful evils

14. **the Western Isles:** the Hebrides (islands off the west coast of Scotland)

15. **kerns and gallowglasses:** i.e., fierce (Irish) soldiers

16. **Fortune:** the goddess Fortuna (See pictures, pages 44, 110, 188.)   **damnèd quarrel:** the accursed cause (for which he fought)

17. **Showed ... whore:** appeared to have granted the rebellious Macdonwald her favors; **all's:** everything (that Macdonwald and Fortune can do) is

21. **Valor's minion:** the chosen darling of Valor

22. **slave:** villain (i.e., Macdonwald)

24. **unseamed ... chops:** ripped him open from his navel to his jaw

(continued)

Scene 2

Alarum within. Enter King ⌜Duncan,⌝ Malcolm, Donalbain, Lennox, with Attendants, meeting a bleeding Captain.

DUNCAN
What bloody man is that? He can report,
As seemeth by his plight, of the revolt
The newest state.
MALCOLM   This is the sergeant
Who, like a good and hardy soldier, fought   5
'Gainst my captivity.—Hail, brave friend!
Say to the King the knowledge of the broil
As thou didst leave it.
CAPTAIN   Doubtful it stood,
As two spent swimmers that do cling together   10
And choke their art. The merciless Macdonwald
(Worthy to be a rebel, for to that
The multiplying villainies of nature
Do swarm upon him) from the Western Isles
Of kerns and ⌜gallowglasses⌝ is supplied;   15
And Fortune, on his damnèd ⌜quarrel⌝ smiling,
Showed like a rebel's whore. But all's too weak;
For brave Macbeth (well he deserves that name),
Disdaining Fortune, with his brandished steel,
Which smoked with bloody execution,   20
Like Valor's minion, carved out his passage
Till he faced the slave;
Which ne'er shook hands, nor bade farewell to him,
Till he unseamed him from the nave to th' chops,
And fixed his head upon our battlements.   25
DUNCAN
O valiant cousin, worthy gentleman!
CAPTAIN
As whence the sun 'gins his reflection
Shipwracking storms and direful thunders ⌜break,⌝

27–28. **As ... break:** i.e., just **as** the east, from which the sun's rays first appear, also brings **storms** (Shakespeare more than once uses *reflect* to describe the sun's emission of rays.)

29. **spring:** source

34. **the Norweyan lord:** i.e., the king of Norway; **surveying vantage:** seeing his chance

40. **say sooth:** speak truthfully

41. **overcharged:** overloaded; **cracks:** i.e., explosive charges

43. **Except:** unless

44. **memorize another Golgotha:** make the event (or place) memorable by turning it into a second Golgotha **Golgotha:** "the place of dead men's skulls" (Mark 15.22) where Jesus was crucified

48. **smack:** have the flavor, taste

50. **Thane:** a title used in Scotland as the equivalent of "baron"

52. **should he:** is one likely to

57. **flout:** mock

Golgotha. (1.2.44)
From Martin Luther, *Ein Sermon* (1523).

So from that spring whence comfort seemed to
  come 30
Discomfort swells. Mark, King of Scotland, mark:
No sooner justice had, with valor armed,
Compelled these skipping kerns to trust their heels,
But the Norweyan lord, surveying vantage,
With furbished arms and new supplies of men, 35
Began a fresh assault.
DUNCAN
  Dismayed not this our captains, Macbeth and
    Banquo?
CAPTAIN
  Yes, as sparrows eagles, or the hare the lion.
  If I say sooth, I must report they were 40
  As cannons overcharged with double cracks,
  So they doubly redoubled strokes upon the foe.
  Except they meant to bathe in reeking wounds
  Or memorize another Golgotha,
  I cannot tell— 45
  But I am faint. My gashes cry for help.
DUNCAN
  So well thy words become thee as thy wounds:
  They smack of honor both.—Go, get him surgeons.
       ⌜*The Captain is led off by Attendants.*⌝

       Enter Ross and Angus.

  Who comes here?
MALCOLM   The worthy Thane of Ross. 50
LENNOX
  What a haste looks through his eyes!
  So should he look that seems to speak things
    strange.
ROSS God save the King.
DUNCAN Whence cam'st thou, worthy thane? 55
ROSS From Fife, great king,
  Where the Norweyan banners flout the sky

58. **people:** i.e., troops
59. **Norway himself:** i.e., the king of **Norway**
61. **dismal:** ominous
62. **Bellona:** Roman goddess of war (Her **bridegroom** would be the fiercest of warriors.) **lapped in proof:** dressed in proven armor
63. **him:** the king of Norway (See longer note, page 193.) **self-comparisons:** (attacks) that matched his own
65. **lavish:** unrestrained
69. **Norways':** Norwegians'; **craves composition:** asks for terms of peace
71. **Saint Colme's Inch:** i.e., Inchcolm, a small island in the Firth of Forth   **Colme's:** pronounced "kollums."
73–74. **deceive / Our bosom interest:** betray my dearest concerns   **Our:** i.e., my (the royal "we")
74. **present:** immediate

1.3 The three witches greet Macbeth as "Thane of Glamis" (as he is), "Thane of Cawdor," and "king hereafter." They then promise Banquo that he will father kings, and they disappear. Almost as soon as they are gone, Ross and Angus arrive with news that the king has named Macbeth "Thane of Cawdor." Macbeth contemplates killing Duncan in order to become "king hereafter" as the witches have called him.

---

7. **Aroint thee:** begone; **rump-fed:** fed on rump meat; fat-rumped; **runnion:** term of abuse for a woman (a Shakespearean coinage used here and in *Merry Wives of Windsor* [4.2.185])

12

And fan our people cold.
Norway himself, with terrible numbers,
Assisted by that most disloyal traitor, 60
The Thane of Cawdor, began a dismal conflict,
Till that Bellona's bridegroom, lapped in proof,
Confronted him with self-comparisons,
Point against point, rebellious arm 'gainst arm,
Curbing his lavish spirit. And to conclude, 65
The victory fell on us.
DUNCAN   Great happiness!
ROSS That now Sweno,
The Norways' king, craves composition.
Nor would we deign him burial of his men 70
Till he disbursèd at Saint Colme's Inch
Ten thousand dollars to our general use.
DUNCAN
No more that Thane of Cawdor shall deceive
Our bosom interest. Go, pronounce his present
 death, 75
And with his former title greet Macbeth.
ROSS I'll see it done.
DUNCAN
What he hath lost, noble Macbeth hath won.
They exit.

Scene 3

Thunder. Enter the three Witches.

FIRST WITCH Where hast thou been, sister?
SECOND WITCH Killing swine.
THIRD WITCH Sister, where thou?
FIRST WITCH
A sailor's wife had chestnuts in her lap
And munched and munched and munched. "Give 5
 me," quoth I.
"Aroint thee, witch," the rump-fed runnion cries.

8. **Tiger:** the name of the sailor's ship
10. **like:** in the form of
15. **the other:** i.e., **the other** winds
16–18. **And ... card:** These lines are variously explained by editors, though all agree that the witch here claims to control the direction and force of the winds (and thus can keep the sailor's ship away from any port). **ports they blow:** perhaps, harbors to which the winds **blow quarters:** i.e., geographical directions **card:** compass **card** or chart (See picture of winds, below.)
21. **penthouse lid:** eyelid
22. **forbid:** under a curse
25. **bark:** ship; **lost:** destroyed
29. **pilot:** helmsman
30. **Wracked:** wrecked; also, tormented
33. **Weïrd:** fateful, fate-determining (In the Folio, the spelling is "weyward" or "weyard.") **Weïrd** is the Scottish form of *wyrd*, the Old English word for fate or destiny.
34. **Posters:** those who post, i.e., travel rapidly

The winds. (1.3.12–18)
From Giulio Cesare Capaccio, *Delle imprese trattato* ... (1592).

14

Her husband's to Aleppo gone, master o' th' *Tiger*;
But in a sieve I'll thither sail,
And, like a rat without a tail, 10
I'll do, I'll do, and I'll do.
SECOND WITCH
 I'll give thee a wind.
FIRST WITCH
 Th' art kind.
THIRD WITCH
 And I another.
FIRST WITCH
 I myself have all the other, 15
 And the very ports they blow;
 All the quarters that they know
 I' th' shipman's card.
 I'll drain him dry as hay.
 Sleep shall neither night nor day 20
 Hang upon his penthouse lid.
 He shall live a man forbid.
 Weary sev'nnights, nine times nine,
 Shall he dwindle, peak, and pine.
 Though his bark cannot be lost, 25
 Yet it shall be tempest-tossed.
 Look what I have.
SECOND WITCH Show me, show me.
FIRST WITCH
 Here I have a pilot's thumb,
 Wracked as homeward he did come. *Drum within.* 30
THIRD WITCH
 A drum, a drum!
 Macbeth doth come.
ALL, ⌜*dancing in a circle*⌝
 The Weïrd Sisters, hand in hand,
 Posters of the sea and land,
 Thus do go about, about, 35
 Thrice to thine and thrice to mine

38. **wound up:** coiled (i.e., like a spring ready for action)
39. **have not seen: have** never **seen** before
40. **is 't called:** is it said to be
46. **choppy:** chapped; or, deeply wrinkled
47. **should be:** must **be** (i.e., most of your features indicate that you are)
56. **fantastical:** figments of the imagination
58. **present grace:** i.e., the title of "Thane of Glamis," already possessed by Macbeth
59. **noble having:** i.e., possession **of noble** titles; **royal hope: hope** of **royal** status
60. **That he seems rapt withal:** so **that he seems** transported by it all
63–64. **neither . . . hate:** neither beg your favors nor fear your hate

Hautboy. (1.6.0 SD)
From Balthasar Küchler, *Repraesentatio* . . . (1611).

And thrice again, to make up nine.
Peace, the charm's wound up.

Enter Macbeth and Banquo.

MACBETH
So foul and fair a day I have not seen.
BANQUO
How far is 't called to ⌜Forres?⌝—What are these, 40
So withered, and so wild in their attire,
That look not like th' inhabitants o' th' Earth
And yet are on 't?—Live you? Or are you aught
That man may question? You seem to understand
  me 45
By each at once her choppy finger laying
Upon her skinny lips. You should be women,
And yet your beards forbid me to interpret
That you are so.
MACBETH   Speak if you can. What are you? 50
FIRST WITCH
All hail, Macbeth! Hail to thee, Thane of Glamis!
SECOND WITCH
All hail, Macbeth! Hail to thee, Thane of Cawdor!
THIRD WITCH
All hail, Macbeth, that shalt be king hereafter!
BANQUO
Good sir, why do you start and seem to fear
Things that do sound so fair?—I' th' name of truth, 55
Are you fantastical, or that indeed
Which outwardly you show? My noble partner
You greet with present grace and great prediction
Of noble having and of royal hope,
That he seems rapt withal. To me you speak not. 60
If you can look into the seeds of time
And say which grain will grow and which will not,
Speak, then, to me, who neither beg nor fear
Your favors nor your hate.

69. **happy:** fortunate
70. **get:** beget, father
73. **imperfect speakers:** i.e., those who speak cryptically or in riddles
74. **Sinel:** Macbeth's father
79. **owe:** own
87. **insane root:** plant that causes insanity

Macbeth and Banquo meet the witches. (1.3.40–81).
From Raphael Holinshed, *The historie of Scotland* (1577).

FIRST WITCH Hail!
SECOND WITCH Hail!
THIRD WITCH Hail!
FIRST WITCH
  Lesser than Macbeth and greater.
SECOND WITCH
  Not so happy, yet much happier.
THIRD WITCH
  Thou shalt get kings, though thou be none.
  So all hail, Macbeth and Banquo!
FIRST WITCH
  Banquo and Macbeth, all hail!
MACBETH
  Stay, you imperfect speakers. Tell me more.
  By Sinel's death I know I am Thane of Glamis.
  But how of Cawdor? The Thane of Cawdor lives
  A prosperous gentleman, and to be king
  Stands not within the prospect of belief,   *doubt*
  No more than to be Cawdor. Say from whence
  You owe this strange intelligence or why
  Upon this blasted heath you stop our way
  With such prophetic greeting. Speak, I charge you.
                                Witches vanish.
BANQUO
  The earth hath bubbles, as the water has,
  And these are of them. Whither are they vanished?
MACBETH
  Into the air, and what seemed corporal melted,
  As breath into the wind. Would they had stayed!
BANQUO
  Were such things here as we do speak about?
  Or have we eaten on the insane root
  That takes the reason prisoner?
MACBETH
  Your children shall be kings.
BANQUO   You shall be king.

93. **happily:** with satisfaction
96–97. **His wonders . . . his:** i.e., the wonder he feels, which makes him speechless, vies with his desire to offer praise (Since he is **silenced** [line 97], his wonder wins the battle.)
99. **stout:** fierce, formidable
101. **Strange . . . death: death** in **strange** forms
101–2. **As thick . . . post:** couriers arrived as rapidly as they could be counted   **tale:** count
107. **herald:** usher
109. **earnest:** a small payment to seal a bargain; thus, a promise **of a greater** reward to come
111. **addition:** title
116. **Who:** he who
119. **combined:** in conspiracy

Heads of traitors "fixed . . . upon" London Bridge. (1.2.25)
From Claes Jansz Visscher, *Londinum florentissima Britanniae urbs* . . . [c. 1625].

MACBETH
  And Thane of Cawdor too. Went it not so?
BANQUO
  To th' selfsame tune and words.—Who's here?

Enter Ross and Angus.

ROSS
  The King hath happily received, Macbeth,
  The news of thy success, and, when he reads
  Thy personal venture in the rebels' fight,   95
  His wonders and his praises do contend
  Which should be thine or his. Silenced with that,
  In viewing o'er the rest o' th' selfsame day
  He finds thee in the stout Norweyan ranks,
  Nothing afeard of what thyself didst make,   100
  Strange images of death. As thick as tale
  ⌜Came⌝ post with post, and every one did bear
  Thy praises in his kingdom's great defense,
  And poured them down before him.
ANGUS   We are sent   105
  To give thee from our royal master thanks,
  Only to herald thee into his sight,
  Not pay thee.
ROSS
  And for an earnest of a greater honor,
  He bade me, from him, call thee Thane of Cawdor,   110
  In which addition, hail, most worthy thane,
  For it is thine.
BANQUO   What, can the devil speak true?
MACBETH
  The Thane of Cawdor lives. Why do you dress me
  In borrowed robes?   115
ANGUS   Who was the Thane lives yet,
  But under heavy judgment bears that life
  Which he deserves to lose. Whether he was
    combined

120. **line the rebel:** i.e., reinforce Macdonwald
126. **The greatest is behind:** the greater part of the prophecy is already accomplished
132. **home:** i.e., fully
133. **enkindle you unto:** inflame you with hope for
137. **betray 's: betray** us
141. **happy:** fortunate
143. **soliciting:** seduction, temptation
144. **ill:** evil
148. **unfix my hair:** make **my hair** stand on end
149. **seated:** i.e., fixed in its place
150. **Against . . . nature:** unnaturally **use:** custom; **Present fears:** causes of fear that are **present**
151. **horrible imaginings:** imaginary horrors
152. **fantastical:** imaginary
154. **function:** ability to act; **surmise:** speculation
155. **but:** except

A crossbow. (1.7.70)
From Wilhelm Dilich, . . . *Krieges-Schule* . . . (1689).

With those of Norway, or did line the rebel 120
With hidden help and vantage, or that with both
He labored in his country's wrack, I know not;
But treasons capital, confessed and proved,
Have overthrown him.
MACBETH, ⌜aside⌝   Glamis and Thane of Cawdor! 125
The greatest is behind. ⌜To Ross and Angus.⌝ Thanks
   for your pains.
⌜Aside to Banquo.⌝ Do you not hope your children
   shall be kings,
When those that gave the Thane of Cawdor to me 130
Promised no less to them?
BANQUO   That, trusted home,
Might yet enkindle you unto the crown,
Besides the Thane of Cawdor. But 'tis strange.
And oftentimes, to win us to our harm, 135
The instruments of darkness tell us truths,
Win us with honest trifles, to betray 's
In deepest consequence.—
Cousins, a word, I pray you.   ⌜They step aside.⌝
MACBETH, ⌜aside⌝   Two truths are told 140
As happy prologues to the swelling act
Of the imperial theme.—I thank you, gentlemen.
⌜Aside.⌝ This supernatural soliciting
Cannot be ill, cannot be good. If ill,
Why hath it given me earnest of success 145
Commencing in a truth? I am Thane of Cawdor.
If good, why do I yield to that suggestion
Whose horrid image doth unfix my hair
And make my seated heart knock at my ribs
Against the use of nature? Present fears 150
Are less than horrible imaginings.
My thought, whose murder yet is but fantastical,
Shakes so my single state of man
That function is smothered in surmise,
And nothing is but what is not. 155

159. **stir:** stirring; taking action
161. **our strange garments:** i.e., new clothes; **cleave . . . mold:** do not fit the body's form
162. **But:** except
164. **Time . . . day:** Proverbial: "The longest **day** has an end."
166. **wrought:** stirred up, affected
172. **The interim having weighed it:** i.e., **having** thought about **it** in **the interim**
172–73. **speak . . . hearts:** i.e., **speak our hearts** freely

1.4 Duncan demands and receives assurances that the former thane of Cawdor has been executed. When Macbeth, Banquo, Ross, and Angus join Duncan, he offers thanks to Macbeth and Banquo. He then announces his intention to have his son Malcolm succeed him as king and his plan to visit Macbeth at Inverness. Macbeth sets out ahead of him to prepare for the royal visit. Now that Malcolm has been named Duncan's successor, Macbeth is convinced that he can become king only by killing Duncan.

0 SD. **Flourish:** fanfare of trumpets
2. **in commission:** i.e., commissioned (to carry out the execution)

BANQUO   Look how our partner's rapt.
MACBETH, ⌜aside⌝
  If chance will have me king, why, chance may
     crown me
  Without my stir.
BANQUO   New honors come upon him,   160
  Like our strange garments, cleave not to their mold
  But with the aid of use.
MACBETH, ⌜aside⌝   Come what come may,
  Time and the hour runs through the roughest day.
BANQUO
  Worthy Macbeth, we stay upon your leisure.   165
MACBETH
  Give me your favor. My dull brain was wrought
  With things forgotten. Kind gentlemen, your pains
  Are registered where every day I turn
  The leaf to read them. Let us toward the King.
  ⌜Aside to Banquo.⌝ Think upon what hath chanced,   170
     and at more time,
  The interim having weighed it, let us speak
  Our free hearts each to other.
BANQUO   Very gladly.
MACBETH   Till then, enough.—Come, friends.   175
                                    They exit.

Scene 4

*Flourish. Enter King ⌜Duncan,⌝ Lennox, Malcolm,
Donalbain, and Attendants.*

DUNCAN
  Is execution done on Cawdor? ⌜Are⌝ not
  Those in commission yet returned?
MALCOLM   My liege,
  They are not yet come back. But I have spoke
  With one that saw him die, who did report   5

11. **owed:** owned
12. **careless:** uncared for, worthless
22–23. **That the proportion . . . mine:** that both my **thanks** and my **payment might have** exceeded what you deserve
24. **all:** i.e., **all** I possess
26. **pays itself:** i.e., is its own reward
27–28. **our duties . . . servants:** i.e., we, as dutiful subjects, owe to you the obligations that **children** owe parents and **servants** owe masters
30. **Safe toward:** protective of

Execution of a Scottish nobleman. (1.4.1–12)
From Raphael Holinshed, *The historie of Scotland* (1577).

That very frankly he confessed his treasons,
Implored your Highness' pardon, and set forth
A deep repentance. Nothing in his life   memory
Became him like the leaving it. He died
As one that had been studied in his death   10
To throw away the dearest thing he owed
As 'twere a careless trifle.
DUNCAN   There's no art
  To find the mind's construction in the face.
He was a gentleman on whom I built   15
An absolute trust.

    Enter Macbeth, Banquo, Ross, and Angus.

               O worthiest cousin,
The sin of my ingratitude even now
Was heavy on me. Thou art so far before
That swiftest wing of recompense is slow   20
To overtake thee. Would thou hadst less deserved,
That the proportion both of thanks and payment
Might have been mine! Only I have left to say,
More is thy due than more than all can pay.
MACBETH
  The service and the loyalty I owe   25
  In doing it pays itself. Your Highness' part
  Is to receive our duties, and our duties
  Are to your throne and state children and servants,
  Which do but what they should by doing everything
  Safe toward your love and honor.   30
DUNCAN   Welcome hither.
  I have begun to plant thee and will labor
  To make thee full of growing.—Noble Banquo,
  That hast no less deserved nor must be known
  No less to have done so, let me enfold thee   35
  And hold thee to my heart.
BANQUO   There, if I grow,
  The harvest is your own.

40. **Wanton:** unrestrained
42. **places:** positions, standing; **nearest:** i.e., closest to the kingship
43. **We . . . upon:** i.e., I name as my heir
44. **hereafter:** henceforth, from now on
45. **Prince of Cumberland:** heir to the throne
46. **Not . . . only:** i.e., **not** be bestowed on him without accompanying honors to others
48. **Inverness:** Macbeth's castle
50. **rest:** leisure, repose
51. **harbinger:** one who is sent before to procure lodging for an army or a royal train
59. **The eye . . . hand:** i.e., let my **eye** not see what my **hand** does
61. **full so valiant:** perhaps, quite as **valiant** as you have said him to be (If this is the correct reading, Duncan is here responding to a comment made to him by Banquo during Macbeth's "aside.")
62. **his commendations:** the praises given him
64. **before:** ahead

A serpent lurking in a strawberry plant. (1.5.76–78)
From Claude Paradin, *The heroicall deuises of* . . . (1591).

Macbeth ACT 1. SC. 4

DUNCAN My plenteous joys,
Wanton in fullness, seek to hide themselves 40
In drops of sorrow.—Sons, kinsmen, thanes,
And you whose places are the nearest, know
We will establish our estate upon
Our eldest, Malcolm, whom we name hereafter
The Prince of Cumberland; which honor must 45
Not unaccompanied invest him only,
But signs of nobleness, like stars, shall shine
On all deservers.—From hence to Inverness
And bind us further to you.
MACBETH
The rest is labor which is not used for you. 50
I'll be myself the harbinger and make joyful
The hearing of my wife with your approach.
So humbly take my leave.
DUNCAN My worthy Cawdor.
MACBETH, ⌜aside⌝
The Prince of Cumberland! That is a step 55
On which I must fall down or else o'erleap,
For in my way it lies. Stars, hide your fires;
Let not light see my black and deep desires.
The eye wink at the hand, yet let that be
Which the eye fears, when it is done, to see. 60
  He exits.
DUNCAN
True, worthy Banquo. He is full so valiant,
And in his commendations I am fed:
It is a banquet to me.—Let's after him,
Whose care is gone before to bid us welcome.
It is a peerless kinsman. 65
  Flourish. They exit.

1.5 Lady Macbeth reads her husband's letter about his meeting the witches. She fears that Macbeth lacks the ruthlessness he needs to kill Duncan and fulfill the witches' second prophecy. When she learns that Duncan is coming to visit, she calls upon supernatural agents to fill her with cruelty. Macbeth arrives, and Lady Macbeth tells him that she will take charge of the preparations for Duncan's visit and for his murder.

---

12. **dues of rejoicing:** i.e., the due measure of joy
16. **fear:** worry about
18. **catch:** take; **nearest way:** shortest route; **wouldst:** wish to
20. **illness:** i.e., ruthlessness
20–21. **wouldst highly:** would greatly like (to have); also, would like to do ambitiously—or idealistically
22. **wouldst thou holily:** would like (to do) in a saintly way
23–28. **Thou'd'st . . . undone:** Lady Macbeth's avoidance of such terms as "murder" and "assassination" leads to imprecise use of **that** and **it.**
28. **should be undone:** i.e., **should** not **be** done
29. **spirits:** vital power, energy
30. **chastise:** rebuke; also, inflict punishment on
31. **the golden round:** i.e., the crown
32. **metaphysical:** supernatural
33. **withal:** i.e., with

Scene 5

Enter Macbeth's Wife, alone, with a letter.

LADY MACBETH, ⌜*reading the letter*⌝ *They met me in the day of success, and I have learned by the perfect'st report they have more in them than mortal knowledge. When I burned in desire to question them further, they made themselves air, into which they vanished. Whiles I stood rapt in the wonder of it came missives from the King, who all-hailed me "Thane of Cawdor," by which title, before, these Weïrd Sisters saluted me and referred me to the coming on of time with "Hail, king that shalt be." This have I thought good to deliver thee, my dearest partner of greatness, that thou might'st not lose the dues of rejoicing by being ignorant of what greatness is promised thee. Lay it to thy heart, and farewell.*

Glamis thou art, and Cawdor, and shalt be
What thou art promised. Yet do I fear thy nature;
It is too full o' th' milk of human kindness
To catch the nearest way. Thou wouldst be great,
Art not without ambition, but without
The illness should attend it. What thou wouldst highly,
That wouldst thou holily; wouldst not play false
And yet wouldst wrongly win. Thou'd'st have, great Glamis,
That which cries "Thus thou must do," if thou have it,
And that which rather thou dost fear to do,
Than wishest should be undone. Hie thee hither,
That I may pour my spirits in thine ear
And chastise with the valor of my tongue
All that impedes thee from the golden round,
Which fate and metaphysical aid doth seem
To have thee crowned withal.

37. **were 't so:** i.e., if the king were coming
38. **informed for preparation:** sent word so that we could be prepared
40. **had the speed of him:** outrode him
43. **Give him tending:** tend to (take care of) him
46. **fatal:** (1) directed by fate; (2) **fatal** to Duncan
48. **mortal:** deadly
49. **crown:** top of the head
51. **remorse:** compassion
52. **compunctious:** remorseful; **visitings:** promptings; **nature:** natural feelings
53. **fell:** cruel; deadly
53–54. **keep . . . it:** i.e., prevent my purpose from having its effect
55. **take . . . gall:** i.e., turn **my milk** into **gall** (i.e., bile, the bitter liquid secreted by the liver and associated with choler or anger); **ministers:** agents
56. **sightless:** invisible
57. **wait on:** attend; also, perhaps, lie in wait for, or accompany; **mischief:** evil
58. **pall thee:** cover yourself as with a pall, a cloth that is put over a coffin; **dunnest:** darkest
63. **all-hail hereafter:** i.e., future kingship

Enter Messenger.

What is your tidings?

MESSENGER
The King comes here tonight. 35
LADY MACBETH Thou 'rt mad to say it.
Is not thy master with him, who, were 't so,
Would have informed for preparation?
MESSENGER
So please you, it is true. Our thane is coming.
One of my fellows had the speed of him, 40
Who, almost dead for breath, had scarcely more
Than would make up his message.
LADY MACBETH Give him tending.
He brings great news. *Messenger exits.*
    The raven himself is hoarse 45
That croaks the fatal entrance of Duncan
Under my battlements. Come, you spirits
That tend on mortal thoughts, unsex me here,
And fill me from the crown to the toe top-full
Of direst cruelty. Make thick my blood. 50
Stop up th' access and passage to remorse,
That no compunctious visitings of nature
Shake my fell purpose, nor keep peace between
Th' effect and it. Come to my woman's breasts
And take my milk for gall, you murd'ring ministers, 55
Wherever in your sightless substances
You wait on nature's mischief. Come, thick night,
And pall thee in the dunnest smoke of hell,
That my keen knife see not the wound it makes,
Nor heaven peep through the blanket of the dark 60
To cry "Hold, hold!"

Enter Macbeth.

    Great Glamis, worthy Cawdor,
Greater than both by the all-hail hereafter!

64. **letters have:** letter has
65. **ignorant:** unknowing
66. **instant:** present moment
74. **beguile the time:** deceive those around us
76–78. **Look like... under 't:** See picture, page 28.
80. **dispatch:** management (with a secondary sense of "putting to death")
82. **solely sovereign:** absolute; **sway:** power
84. **look up clear: look** cheerful and undisturbed
85. **To alter... fear:** perhaps, a changed countenance frightens others; or, perhaps, when one is fearful one's countenance always changes **favor:** countenance, face

1.6 Duncan and his attendants arrive at Inverness. Lady Macbeth welcomes them.

———

0 SD. **Hautboys:** powerful double-reed woodwind instruments, also called "shawms," designed for outdoor ceremonials (Oboes are later descendants of hautboys, with a much softer tone.) See picture, page 16.
1. **seat:** site, situation

  Thy letters have transported me beyond
  This ignorant present, and I feel now   65
  The future in the instant.
MACBETH   My dearest love,
  Duncan comes here tonight.
LADY MACBETH   And when goes hence?
MACBETH
  Tomorrow, as he purposes.   70
LADY MACBETH   O, never
  Shall sun that morrow see!
  Your face, my thane, is as a book where men
  May read strange matters. To beguile the time,
  Look like the time. Bear welcome in your eye, 75
  Your hand, your tongue. Look like th' innocent
    flower,
  But be the serpent under 't. He that's coming
  Must be provided for; and you shall put
  This night's great business into my dispatch, 80
  Which shall to all our nights and days to come
  Give solely sovereign sway and masterdom.
MACBETH
  We will speak further.
LADY MACBETH   Only look up clear.
  To alter favor ever is to fear.   85
  Leave all the rest to me.
              They exit.

Scene 6

Hautboys and Torches. Enter King ⌜Duncan,⌝ Malcolm, Donalbain, Banquo, Lennox, Macduff, Ross, Angus, and Attendants.

DUNCAN
  This castle hath a pleasant seat. The air
  Nimbly and sweetly recommends itself
  Unto our gentle senses.

5. **martlet:** house martin; **approve:** demonstrate
6. **By his loved mansionry:** i.e., by the fact that he loves to build nests here
7. **wooingly:** invitingly; **jutty:** projection
8. **coign of vantage:** i.e., protruding corner of **vantage:** affording a good observation point
9. **pendant:** hanging, suspended; **procreant cradle:** cradle where he breeds

14–15. **The love ... as love:** perhaps, uninvited attention from someone who loves us can be troublesome, but we are grateful for it as a sign of **love** (These lines are difficult, in part, because Duncan's use of **us** could mean "me" [the royal plural] or could indicate a generalization, as we here interpret it.)

15–17. **Herein ... trouble:** i.e., in saying this, **I teach you how** to say "thank you" **for** the **trouble** I'm causing you, since it is the result of my love **God 'ild:** God yield (i.e., thank you)

20. **single:** trivial

20–21. **contend / Against:** rival, try to match

22. **those:** i.e., **those** honors

23. **late:** recent; **heaped up:** added

24. **We rest your hermits:** we remain your beadsmen (Beadsmen repaid gifts with prayers for the donor. See picture, page 114.)

26. **We:** i.e., I (royal plural); **coursed:** pursued

27. **purveyor:** a servant who makes advance preparations for a noble master

33. **theirs:** i.e., their dependents; **what is theirs:** what they own; **in compt:** in trust (from the king)

35. **Still:** always

BANQUO   This guest of summer,
  The temple-haunting ⌈martlet,⌉ does approve,   5
  By his loved ⌈mansionry,⌉ that the heaven's breath
  Smells wooingly here. No jutty, frieze,
  Buttress, nor coign of vantage, but this bird
  Hath made his pendant bed and procreant cradle.
  Where they ⌈most⌉ breed and haunt, I have   10
     observed,
  The air is delicate.

                    Enter Lady ⌈Macbeth.⌉

DUNCAN   See, see our honored hostess!—
  The love that follows us sometime is our trouble,
  Which still we thank as love. Herein I teach you   15
  How you shall bid God 'ild us for your pains
  And thank us for your trouble.
LADY MACBETH   All our service,
  In every point twice done and then done double,
  Were poor and single business to contend   20
  Against those honors deep and broad wherewith
  Your Majesty loads our house. For those of old,
  And the late dignities heaped up to them,
  We rest your hermits.
DUNCAN   Where's the Thane of Cawdor?   25
  We coursed him at the heels and had a purpose
  To be his purveyor; but he rides well,
  And his great love, sharp as his spur, hath helped
     him
  To his home before us. Fair and noble hostess,   30
  We are your guest tonight.
LADY MACBETH   Your servants ever
  Have theirs, themselves, and what is theirs in compt
  To make their audit at your Highness' pleasure,
  Still to return your own.   35
DUNCAN   Give me your hand.

1.7 Macbeth contemplates the reasons why it is a terrible thing to kill Duncan. Lady Macbeth mocks his fears and offers a plan for Duncan's murder, which Macbeth accepts.

0 SD. **Sewer:** butler; **service:** i.e., food
1–2. **If . . . quickly:** This sentence plays with several meanings of **done** (finished with, accomplished, performed) and for the moment leaves **it** unspecified.
3. **trammel up:** catch as in a net (See picture, page 40.)
4. **his surcease:** Duncan's death; or its (the assassination's) completion; **that but:** if only
7. **jump the life to come:** risk the fate of my soul
17. **Hath . . . meek:** has exercised his power so humbly (or so compassionately)
18. **clear:** blameless
19. **plead:** argue (as in a court of law)
20. **taking-off:** i.e., murder
22. **Striding the blast:** riding the wind; **cherubin:** angel (See longer note, page 193.)

⌜*Taking her hand.*⌝
Conduct me to mine host. We love him highly
And shall continue our graces towards him.
By your leave, hostess.

They exit.

Scene 7

Hautboys. Torches. Enter a Sewer and divers Servants with dishes and service over the stage. Then enter Macbeth.

MACBETH
If it were done when 'tis done, then 'twere well
It were done quickly. If th' assassination
Could trammel up the consequence and catch
With his surcease success, that but this blow
Might be the be-all and the end-all here, 5
But here, upon this bank and ⌜shoal⌝ of time,
We'd jump the life to come. But in these cases
We still have judgment here, that we but teach
Bloody instructions, which, being taught, return
To plague th' inventor. This even-handed justice 10
Commends th' ingredience of our poisoned chalice
To our own lips. He's here in double trust:
First, as I am his kinsman and his subject,
Strong both against the deed; then, as his host,
Who should against his murderer shut the door, 15
Not bear the knife myself. Besides, this Duncan
Hath borne his faculties so meek, hath been
So clear in his great office, that his virtues
Will plead like angels, trumpet-tongued, against
The deep damnation of his taking-off; 20
And pity, like a naked newborn babe
Striding the blast, or heaven's cherubin horsed

23. **sightless couriers:** invisible or unseen coursers or steeds

25. **That:** so **that; tears shall drown the wind:** i.e., **tears** as thick as rain will still **the wind**

27. **which o'erleaps itself:** i.e., **which,** in leaping into the saddle, jumps too far

35. **bought:** acquired

37. **would be:** ought to **be,** wish to **be**

41. **green and pale:** sickly, as if hung over from drinking

43. **Such:** i.e., fickle, like his hope and resolution

48. **wait upon:** always follow, accompany

49. **the poor cat i' th' adage:** i.e., **the cat** who would eat fish but would not get its feet wet (proverbial)   **adage:** proverb

52. **none:** i.e., not **a man** (line 51)

A trammel net. (1.7.3)
From *Fables d'Esope* (1678).

Upon the sightless couriers of the air,
Shall blow the horrid deed in every eye,
That tears shall drown the wind. I have no spur   25
To prick the sides of my intent, but only
Vaulting ambition, which o'erleaps itself
And falls on th' other—

Enter Lady ⌈Macbeth.⌉

How now, what news?
LADY MACBETH
He has almost supped. Why have you left the   30
  chamber?
MACBETH
Hath he asked for me?
LADY MACBETH   Know you not he has?
MACBETH
We will proceed no further in this business.
He hath honored me of late, and I have bought   35
Golden opinions from all sorts of people,
Which would be worn now in their newest gloss,
Not cast aside so soon.
LADY MACBETH   Was the hope drunk
Wherein you dressed yourself? Hath it slept since?   40
And wakes it now, to look so green and pale
At what it did so freely? From this time
Such I account thy love. Art thou afeard
To be the same in thine own act and valor
As thou art in desire? Wouldst thou have that   45
Which thou esteem'st the ornament of life
And live a coward in thine own esteem,
Letting "I dare not" wait upon "I would,"
Like the poor cat i' th' adage?
MACBETH   Prithee, peace.   50
I dare do all that may become a man.
Who dares ⌈do⌉ more is none.

55. **break:** broach, disclose
56. **durst:** dared
58. **Nor ... nor:** neither ... **nor**
59. **adhere:** agree, conjoin
60. **that their fitness:** their very convenience (for the assassination)
62. **unmake:** i.e., unman, unnerve
70. **But:** only; **screw ... place:** The image may be that of a crossbow string that is mechanically tightened into its notch. (See picture, page 22.)
72. **Whereto the rather:** to which all the sooner
73. **Soundly invite him:** i.e., **invite him** to sleep soundly; **chamberlains:** servants of the bedchamber
74. **wassail:** carousing; **convince:** overpower (Latin *vincere,* "to conquer")
75. **warder:** guardian
76. **receipt of reason:** container that encloses **reason**
77. **limbeck:** alembic (the upper part of a still into which fumes rise)
78. **drenchèd natures:** drowned faculties
80. **put upon:** impute to, blame on
81. **spongy:** i.e., having soaked up wine
82. **quell:** murder
84. **mettle:** spirit; metal
85. **received:** accepted as true

LADY MACBETH   What beast was 't, then,
That made you break this enterprise to me?   55
When you durst do it, then you were a man;
And to be more than what you were, you would
Be so much more the man. Nor time nor place
Did then adhere, and yet you would make both.
They have made themselves, and that their fitness   60
  now
Does unmake you. I have given suck, and know
How tender 'tis to love the babe that milks me.
I would, while it was smiling in my face,
Have plucked my nipple from his boneless gums   65
And dashed the brains out, had I so sworn as you
Have done to this.
MACBETH   If we should fail—
LADY MACBETH   We fail?
But screw your courage to the sticking place   70
And we'll not fail. When Duncan is asleep
(Whereto the rather shall his day's hard journey
Soundly invite him), his two chamberlains
Will I with wine and wassail so convince
That memory, the warder of the brain,   75
Shall be a fume, and the receipt of reason
A limbeck only. When in swinish sleep
Their drenchèd natures lies as in a death,
What cannot you and I perform upon
Th' unguarded Duncan? What not put upon   80
His spongy officers, who shall bear the guilt
Of our great quell?
MACBETH   Bring forth men-children only,
For thy undaunted mettle should compose
Nothing but males. Will it not be received,   85
When we have marked with blood those sleepy two
Of his own chamber and used their very daggers,
That they have done 't?

89. **other:** otherwise
92. **settled:** determined
92–93. **bend . . . agent:** exert all the power in my body
93. **to:** i.e., to perform
94. **mock:** deceive
95. **False:** deceptive; **false:** treacherous

Fortune. (1.2.16–17, 19)
From George Wither, *A collection of emblemes* . . . (1635).

LADY MACBETH   Who dares receive it other,
   As we shall make our griefs and clamor roar   90
   Upon his death?
MACBETH   I am settled and bend up
   Each corporal agent to this terrible feat.
   Away, and mock the time with fairest show.
   False face must hide what the false heart doth   95
      know.

going to kill Duncan   *They exit.*

The Tragedy of
MACBETH

ACT 2

2.1 Banquo, who has accompanied Duncan to Inverness, is uneasy because he too is tempted by the witches' prophecies, although only in his dreams. Macbeth pretends to have forgotten them. Left alone by Banquo, Macbeth sees a gory dagger leading him to Duncan's room. Hearing the bell rung by Lady Macbeth to signal completion of her preparations for Duncan's death, Macbeth exits to kill the king.

---

6. **husbandry:** careful use of resources, frugality
7. **Take thee that:** perhaps giving Fleance his dagger
8. **heavy summons: summons** to sleep
17. **largess:** gifts, tips; **offices:** i.e., servants

Tarquin and Lucrece. (2.1.67)
From Jost Amman, *Icones Liuianae* (1572).

ACT 2

Scene 1

Enter Banquo, and Fleance with a torch before him.

BANQUO How goes the night, boy?
FLEANCE
  The moon is down. I have not heard the clock.
BANQUO And she goes down at twelve.
FLEANCE I take 't 'tis later, sir.
BANQUO
  Hold, take my sword. ⌜*He gives his sword to Fleance.*⌝   5
         There's husbandry in heaven;
  Their candles are all out. Take thee that too.
  A heavy summons lies like lead upon me,
  And yet I would not sleep. Merciful powers,
  Restrain in me the cursèd thoughts that nature   10
  Gives way to in repose.

   Enter Macbeth, and a Servant with a torch.

                Give me my sword.—Who's
    there?
MACBETH A friend.
BANQUO
  What, sir, not yet at rest? The King's abed.   15
  He hath been in unusual pleasure, and
  Sent forth great largess to your offices.
  This diamond he greets your wife withal,

49

19. **shut up:** concluded (his remarks); or summed up (what he had to say)

22–23. **Our will . . . wrought:** i.e., our desire (to entertain the king properly) was limited (by our lack of time to prepare); otherwise our desire would have operated freely, liberally   **will:** desire   **became the servant to defect:** was subjected to deficiency   **wrought:** operated

29. **entreat an hour to serve:** i.e., find a time that suits us

34. **cleave to my consent:** i.e., support me, join my party   **cleave:** adhere

37. **still:** always, continue to

38. **My bosom franchised:** my inmost being free

39. **I shall be counseled:** I will be willing to listen; or, I will follow your counsel

48. **fatal vision:** an apparition (1) that is ominous or fateful, (2) that represents a deadly weapon, or (3) that shows what is fated, sent by Fate

48–49. **sensible / To feeling:** perceptible to the sense of touch

By the name of most kind hostess, and shut up
In measureless content.   20
                    ⌜*He gives Macbeth a jewel.*⌝
MACBETH   Being unprepared,
  Our will became the servant to defect,
  Which else should free have wrought.
BANQUO   All's well.
  I dreamt last night of the three Weïrd Sisters.   25
  To you they have showed some truth.
MACBETH   I think not of
    them.
  Yet, when we can entreat an hour to serve,
  We would spend it in some words upon that   30
    business,
  If you would grant the time.
BANQUO   At your kind'st leisure.
MACBETH
  If you shall cleave to my consent, when 'tis,
  It shall make honor for you.   35
BANQUO   So I lose none
  In seeking to augment it, but still keep
  My bosom franchised and allegiance clear,
  I shall be counseled.
MACBETH   Good repose the while.   40
BANQUO   Thanks, sir. The like to you.
                    Banquo ⌜*and Fleance*⌝ *exit.*
MACBETH
  Go bid thy mistress, when my drink is ready,
  She strike upon the bell. Get thee to bed.
                              ⌜*Servant*⌝ *exits.*
  Is this a dagger which I see before me,
  The handle toward my hand? Come, let me clutch   45
    thee.
  I have thee not, and yet I see thee still.
  Art thou not, fatal vision, sensible
  To feeling as to sight? Or art thou but

50. **false:** unreal
51. **heat-oppressèd:** feverishly excited
54. **Thou marshal'st:** you lead
56. **made the fools o' th' other senses: made fools of** by the evidence given by my sense of touch
57. **Or else worth all the rest: or else** my eyes alone report the truth
58. **dudgeon:** handle; **gouts:** clots
59. **There's no such thing:** i.e., the dagger does not exist
62. **abuse:** deceive
64. **Hecate's off'rings:** sacrifices offered to Hecate, goddess of the moon and of witchcraft
65. **Alarumed:** summoned to action (*all' arme*, "to arms!")
66. **watch:** i.e., cry, like that of a watchman; **thus:** Macbeth here begins to move **with** the **stealthy pace** of a murderer, toward his design.
67. **Tarquin:** a Roman infamous for his rape of Lucrece (Shakespeare had told the story of the rape and Lucrece's suicide in his *Lucrece* [1594].) **ravishing:** (1) ravenous; (2) leading to rape (See picture, page 48.)
72. **take . . . time: take** away (with the sound of his footsteps) **the horror** of the moment's absolute silence
73. **suits:** agrees, fits in; **threat:** offer threats
74. **Words . . . gives:** i.e., talking simply cools off **the heat** that drives action

A dagger of the mind, a false creation   50
Proceeding from the heat-oppressèd brain?
I see thee yet, in form as palpable
As this which now I draw.   ⌜*He draws his dagger.*⌝
Thou marshal'st me the way that I was going,
And such an instrument I was to use.   55
Mine eyes are made the fools o' th' other senses
Or else worth all the rest. I see thee still,
And, on thy blade and dudgeon, gouts of blood,
Which was not so before. There's no such thing.
It is the bloody business which informs   60
Thus to mine eyes. Now o'er the one-half world
Nature seems dead, and wicked dreams abuse
The curtained sleep. Witchcraft celebrates
Pale Hecate's off'rings, and withered murder,
Alarumed by his sentinel, the wolf,   65
Whose howl's his watch, thus with his stealthy pace,
With Tarquin's ravishing ⌜strides,⌝ towards his
    design
Moves like a ghost. Thou ⌜sure⌝ and firm-set earth,
Hear not my steps, which ⌜way they⌝ walk, for fear   70
Thy very stones prate of my whereabouts
And take the present horror from the time,
Which now suits with it. Whiles I threat, he lives.
Words to the heat of deeds too cold breath gives.
                              A bell rings.
I go, and it is done. The bell invites me.   75
Hear it not, Duncan, for it is a knell
That summons thee to heaven or to hell.
                              He exits.

2.2 Lady Macbeth waits anxiously for Macbeth to return from killing Duncan. When Macbeth enters, he is horrified by what he has done. He has brought with him the daggers that he used on Duncan, instead of leaving them in the room with Duncan's servants as Lady Macbeth had planned. When he finds himself incapable of returning the daggers, Lady Macbeth does so. She returns to find Macbeth still paralyzed with horror and urges him to put on his gown and wash the blood from his hands.

---

5. **bellman:** town crier, who sounded the hours of the night and tolled the bell on the evening before an execution (Here, **the owl** is a bellman because, according to superstition, the hoot of the owl portends death. It is **fatal** perhaps because sent by Fate, or perhaps because it predicts death.) See pictures, pages 56 and 64.
6. **He:** Macbeth
8. **mock their charge:** make a mockery of their responsibility
9. **possets:** hot drinks, containing milk and liquor
15. **Confounds:** ruins
16. **He:** Macbeth; **he:** Duncan

Scene 2

Enter Lady ⌜Macbeth.⌝

LADY MACBETH
That which hath made them drunk hath made me bold.
What hath quenched them hath given me fire.
Hark!—Peace.
It was the owl that shrieked, the fatal bellman,
Which gives the stern'st good-night. He is about it.
The doors are open, and the surfeited grooms
Do mock their charge with snores. I have drugged their possets,
That death and nature do contend about them
Whether they live or die.

MACBETH, ⌜*within*⌝   Who's there? What, ho!

LADY MACBETH
Alack, I am afraid they have awaked,
And 'tis not done. Th' attempt and not the deed
Confounds us. Hark!—I laid their daggers ready;
He could not miss 'em. Had he not resembled
My father as he slept, I had done 't.

Enter Macbeth ⌜with bloody daggers.⌝

My husband?

MACBETH
I have done the deed. Didst thou not hear a noise?

LADY MACBETH
I heard the owl scream and the crickets cry.
Did not you speak?

MACBETH   When?

LADY MACBETH   Now.

MACBETH   As I descended?

LADY MACBETH   Ay.

MACBETH   Hark!—Who lies i' th' second chamber?

LADY MACBETH   Donalbain.

28. **sorry:** deplorable, wretched
34. **addressed them:** applied themselves
38. **As:** as if; **hangman's:** executioner's (The hangman also had to cut the body to pieces, hence his bloody hands.)
39. **List'ning:** i.e., listening to
42. **wherefore:** why
46. **so:** if **so**
47. **Methought:** it seemed to me
49. **knits:** ties; **raveled sleave:** tangled threads
51. **second course:** i.e., main **course**

A bellman. (2.2.5)
From Thomas Dekker, *The belman of London* (1616).

MACBETH This is a sorry sight.
LADY MACBETH
  A foolish thought, to say a sorry sight.
MACBETH
  There's one did laugh in 's sleep, and one cried
    "Murder!"
  That they did wake each other. I stood and heard
    them.
  But they did say their prayers and addressed them
  Again to sleep.
LADY MACBETH There are two lodged together.
MACBETH
  One cried "God bless us" and "Amen" the other,
  As they had seen me with these hangman's hands,
  List'ning their fear. I could not say "Amen"
  When they did say "God bless us."
LADY MACBETH Consider it not so deeply.
MACBETH
  But wherefore could not I pronounce "Amen"?
  I had most need of blessing, and "Amen"
  Stuck in my throat.
LADY MACBETH   These deeds must not be thought
  After these ways; so, it will make us mad.
MACBETH
  Methought I heard a voice cry "Sleep no more!
  Macbeth does murder sleep"—the innocent sleep,
  Sleep that knits up the raveled sleave of care,
  The death of each day's life, sore labor's bath,
  Balm of hurt minds, great nature's second course,
  Chief nourisher in life's feast.
LADY MACBETH   What do you mean?
MACBETH
  Still it cried "Sleep no more!" to all the house.
  "Glamis hath murdered sleep, and therefore
    Cawdor
  Shall sleep no more. Macbeth shall sleep no more."

59. **unbend:** loosen, slacken (contrasts with "bend up" at 1.7.92)
60. **brainsickly:** madly; or, morbidly
61. **witness:** evidence
72. **gild:** i.e., smear; **withal:** with it (i.e., with Duncan's blood)
78. **Neptune:** the Roman god of the sea (See picture, below.)
80. **multitudinous:** vast; **incarnadine:** turn blood-red
81. **one red:** i.e., a uniform red color
82. **shame:** would be ashamed
87. **constancy:** firmness of mind
88. **left you unattended:** abandoned you

Neptune, god of the sea. (2.2.78)
From Vincenzo Cartari, *Imagini delli dei de gl'antichi . . .* (1674).

LADY MACBETH
  Who was it that thus cried? Why, worthy thane,
  You do unbend your noble strength to think
  So brainsickly of things. Go get some water
  And wash this filthy witness from your hand.—
  Why did you bring these daggers from the place?
  They must lie there. Go, carry them and smear
  The sleepy grooms with blood.
MACBETH   I'll go no more.
  I am afraid to think what I have done.
  Look on 't again I dare not.
LADY MACBETH   Infirm of purpose!
  Give me the daggers. The sleeping and the dead
  Are but as pictures. 'Tis the eye of childhood
  That fears a painted devil. If he do bleed,
  I'll gild the faces of the grooms withal,
  For it must seem their guilt.
          She exits ⌜with the daggers.⌝ Knock within.
MACBETH   Whence is that
    knocking?
  How is 't with me when every noise appalls me?
  What hands are here! Ha, they pluck out mine eyes.
  Will all great Neptune's ocean wash this blood
  Clean from my hand? No, this my hand will rather
  The multitudinous seas incarnadine,
  Making the green one red.

          Enter Lady ⌜Macbeth.⌝

LADY MACBETH
  My hands are of your color, but I shame
  To wear a heart so white.   *Knock.*
                       I hear a knocking
  At the south entry. Retire we to our chamber.
  A little water clears us of this deed.
  How easy is it, then! Your constancy
  Hath left you unattended.   *Knock.*

90. **nightgown:** dressing gown; **occasion:** circumstances
91. **show us to be watchers:** reveal that we are still up and awake
92. **poorly:** poor-spiritedly, dispiritedly

2.3 A drunken porter, answering the knocking at the gate, plays the role of a devil-porter at the gates of hell. He admits Macduff and Lennox, who have come to wake Duncan. Macbeth appears and greets them. Macduff exits to wake Duncan, then returns to announce Duncan's murder. Macbeth and Lennox go to see for themselves. When they return, Lennox announces that Duncan's servants are the murderers. Macbeth reveals that he has slain the servants. When his motives are questioned, Lady Macbeth interrupts by calling for help for herself. Duncan's sons, Malcolm and Donalbain, plan to flee for their lives—Malcolm to England, Donalbain to Ireland.

---

0 SD. **Porter:** gatekeeper
2. **old:** i.e., plenty of
4. **Beelzebub:** Matthew 12.24: "Beelzebub, the prince of the devils"
4–5. **farmer...plenty:** perhaps, the **farmer** hoarded crops only to face an unexpected surplus and dropping prices
6. **napkins:** handkerchiefs (to mop up his sweat)
8. **equivocator:** one who intentionally speaks ambiguously, either by using words that can be

(continued)

      Hark, more knocking.
Get on your nightgown, lest occasion call us 90
And show us to be watchers. Be not lost
So poorly in your thoughts.
MACBETH
To know my deed 'twere best not know myself.
           Knock.
Wake Duncan with thy knocking. I would thou
 couldst.   95
          They exit.

Scene 3

Knocking within. Enter a Porter.

PORTER Here's a knocking indeed! If a man were porter of hell gate, he should have old turning the key. *(Knock.)* Knock, knock, knock! Who's there, i' th' name of Beelzebub? Here's a farmer that hanged himself on th' expectation of plenty. Come in time! 5
Have napkins enough about you; here you'll sweat for 't. *(Knock.)* Knock, knock! Who's there, in th' other devil's name? Faith, here's an equivocator that could swear in both the scales against either scale, who committed treason enough for God's 10
sake yet could not equivocate to heaven. O, come in, equivocator. *(Knock.)* Knock, knock, knock! Who's there? Faith, here's an English tailor come hither for stealing out of a French hose. Come in, tailor. Here you may roast your goose. *(Knock.)* Knock, knock! 15
Never at quiet.—What are you?—But this place is too cold for hell. I'll devil-porter it no further. I had thought to have let in some of all professions that go the primrose way to th' everlasting bonfire. *(Knock.)*
Anon, anon!   20

⌜*The Porter opens the door to*⌝ *Macduff and Lennox.*

 I pray you, remember the porter.

taken more than one way or by mentally hedging or limiting his or her words (See longer note, page 194.)

14. **stealing...hose:** perhaps, **stealing** cloth in the process of making breeches

15. **roast your goose:** heat your tailor's iron (**Goose** was also a slang term for prostitute.)

19. **primrose way...bonfire:** the broad and pleasurable path to hell (See Matthew 7.13.)

20. **Anon:** right away

21. **I pray you, remember the porter:** This is a request for a tip.

24–25. **the second cock:** i.e., 3 A.M.

29. **nose-painting:** reddening the nose through drink

37. **giving him the lie:** (1) lying to him; (2) laying him out

40. **i' th' very throat on me:** in my **very throat** (To "give a lie in the throat" was to accuse someone of deep, deliberate lying.) **on:** of

42. **took up my legs:** lifted my feet off the ground (an image from wrestling), perhaps in a drunken stagger

43. **made a shift:** managed; **cast him:** give him a fall (as in wrestling); throw it out (vomit, urinate)

50. **timely:** early

51. **slipped the hour:** allowed **the hour** to slip by

MACDUFF
  Was it so late, friend, ere you went to bed
  That you do lie so late?
PORTER Faith, sir, we were carousing till the second cock, and drink, sir, is a great provoker of three things.
MACDUFF What three things does drink especially provoke?
PORTER Marry, sir, nose-painting, sleep, and urine. Lechery, sir, it provokes and unprovokes. It provokes the desire, but it takes away the performance. Therefore much drink may be said to be an equivocator with lechery. It makes him, and it mars him; it sets him on, and it takes him off; it persuades him and disheartens him; makes him stand to and not stand to; in conclusion, equivocates him in a sleep and, giving him the lie, leaves him.
MACDUFF I believe drink gave thee the lie last night.
PORTER That it did, sir, i' th' very throat on me; but I requited him for his lie, and, I think, being too strong for him, though he took up my legs sometime, yet I made a shift to cast him.
MACDUFF Is thy master stirring?

Enter Macbeth.

Our knocking has awaked him. Here he comes.
⌜*Porter exits.*⌝
LENNOX
  Good morrow, noble sir.
MACBETH   Good morrow, both.
MACDUFF
  Is the King stirring, worthy thane?
MACBETH   Not yet.
MACDUFF
  He did command me to call timely on him.
  I have almost slipped the hour.

55. **physics:** relieves (To *physic* was to treat an illness with physic, or medicine.)
58. **limited service:** appointed duty
60. **appoint:** plan to do
66. **combustion:** tumult, confusion
67. **obscure bird:** bird of darkness, owl (See picture, below.)   **obscure:** accent on first syllable
76. **Confusion:** destruction
78. **The Lord's anointed temple:** the body of the king, which was represented by Renaissance monarchies as having been **anointed** by God

"It was the owl, . . . the fatal bellman."
(2.2.5; see also 2.2.20; 2.3.67–68; and 4.2.13)
From George Wither, *A collection of emblemes* . . . (1635).

MACBETH   I'll bring you to him.
MACDUFF
    I know this is a joyful trouble to you,
    But yet 'tis one.
MACBETH
    The labor we delight in physics pain.   55
    This is the door.
    MACDUFF   I'll make so bold to call,
    For 'tis my limited service.   *Macduff exits.*
LENNOX   Goes the King hence today?
MACBETH   He does. He did appoint so.   60
LENNOX
    The night has been unruly. Where we lay,
    Our chimneys were blown down and, as they say,
    Lamentings heard i' th' air, strange screams of
        death,
    And prophesying, with accents terrible,   65
    Of dire combustion and confused events
    New hatched to th' woeful time. The obscure bird
    Clamored the livelong night. Some say the Earth
    Was feverous and did shake.
MACBETH   'Twas a rough night.   70
LENNOX
    My young remembrance cannot parallel
    A fellow to it.

              Enter Macduff.

MACDUFF   O horror, horror, horror!
    Tongue nor heart cannot conceive nor name thee!
MACBETH and LENNOX   What's the matter?   75
MACDUFF
    Confusion now hath made his masterpiece.
    Most sacrilegious murder hath broke ope
    The Lord's anointed temple and stole thence
    The life o' th' building.

83. **Gorgon:** a mythological figure, the sight of whom brought instant death (See picture, below.)

90. **great doom's image:** a sight as terrible as doomsday

91. **As . . . sprites:** as if, at the Last Judgment, you **rise from your graves like** ghosts

92. **countenance:** be in keeping with

94. **calls to parley:** The image is of the battlefield, where a **parley** is a conference.

98. **repetition:** report, account

Perseus with the Gorgon's head. (2.3.83)
From Cesare Ripa, *Noua iconologia* (1618).

MACBETH   What is 't you say? The life?   80
LENNOX   Mean you his Majesty?
MACDUFF
  Approach the chamber and destroy your sight
  With a new Gorgon. Do not bid me speak.
  See and then speak yourselves.
                    Macbeth and Lennox exit.
                              Awake, awake!   85
  Ring the alarum bell.—Murder and treason!
  Banquo and Donalbain, Malcolm, awake!
  Shake off this downy sleep, death's counterfeit,
  And look on death itself. Up, up, and see
  The great doom's image. Malcolm, Banquo,   90
  As from your graves rise up and walk like sprites
  To countenance this horror.—Ring the bell.
                              Bell rings.

            Enter Lady ⌜Macbeth.⌝

LADY MACBETH   What's the business,
  That such a hideous trumpet calls to parley
  The sleepers of the house? Speak, speak!   95
MACDUFF   O gentle lady,
  'Tis not for you to hear what I can speak.
  The repetition in a woman's ear
  Would murder as it fell.

              Enter Banquo.

                    O Banquo, Banquo,   100
  Our royal master's murdered.
LADY MACBETH   Woe, alas!
  What, in our house?
BANQUO   Too cruel anywhere.—
  Dear Duff, I prithee, contradict thyself   105
  And say it is not so.

107. **but:** only; **chance:** occurrence
109. **nothing serious in mortality:** nothing important in life
110. **toys:** trifles; **grace:** honor
111–12. **The wine . . . brag of:** i.e., the **vault** has had the wine **drawn** off and nothing **is left** but the dregs (**lees**)
113–14. **What is amiss? / You are:** i.e., "What is wrong (**amiss**)?" "You are damaged (**amiss**) in that your father is killed."
115. **head:** fountainhead, source
120. **badged:** marked, as with badges
122. **distracted:** distraught
126. **Wherefore:** why
127. **amazed:** utterly confused, bewildered
128. **in a moment:** simultaneously
129. **expedition:** haste
132. **breach:** gap (technically, a break in a fortification caused by battering)
133. **wasteful:** destructive

Enter Macbeth, Lennox, and Ross.

MACBETH
  Had I but died an hour before this chance,
  I had lived a blessèd time; for from this instant
  There's nothing serious in mortality.
  All is but toys. Renown and grace is dead.   110
  The wine of life is drawn, and the mere lees
  Is left this vault to brag of.

Enter Malcolm and Donalbain.

DONALBAIN What is amiss?
MACBETH You are, and do not know 't.
  The spring, the head, the fountain of your blood   115
  Is stopped; the very source of it is stopped.
MACDUFF
  Your royal father's murdered.
MALCOLM   O, by whom?
LENNOX
  Those of his chamber, as it seemed, had done 't.
  Their hands and faces were all badged with blood.   120
  So were their daggers, which unwiped we found
  Upon their pillows. They stared and were distracted.
  No man's life was to be trusted with them.
MACBETH
  O, yet I do repent me of my fury,
  That I did kill them.   125
MACDUFF   Wherefore did you so?
MACBETH
  Who can be wise, amazed, temp'rate, and furious,
  Loyal, and neutral, in a moment? No man.
  Th' expedition of my violent love
  Outrun the pauser, reason. Here lay Duncan,   130
  His silver skin laced with his golden blood,
  And his gashed stabs looked like a breach in nature
  For ruin's wasteful entrance; there the murderers,

134. **Steeped:** soaked
135. **Unmannerly breeched with gore:** i.e., improperly clothed with blood (instead of being properly sheathed); **refrain:** hold himself back
137. **make 's: make** his
138. **Help me hence, ho!:** Lady Macbeth perhaps faints—or pretends to faint—at this point.
142. **That . . . ours:** i.e., that have the best right to speak on this subject
144. **Hid in an auger hole:** concealed in a tiny crack (i.e., hiding in ambush)
146. **upon the foot of motion:** ready to move, to take action
148. **naked frailties hid:** i.e., clothed our frail bodies
150. **question:** examine
151. **scruples:** suspicions
153–54. **Against . . . malice:** i.e., **I fight against the** unrevealed purpose of the traitor
157. **briefly:** quickly; **put on manly readiness:** clothe ourselves properly (with perhaps also a sense of emotional readiness)
160. **consort:** join in league
161. **office:** function

Steeped in the colors of their trade, their daggers
Unmannerly breeched with gore. Who could refrain   135
That had a heart to love, and in that heart
Courage to make 's love known?
LADY MACBETH   Help me hence, ho!
MACDUFF
  Look to the lady.
MALCOLM, ⌜*aside to Donalbain*⌝   Why do we hold our   140
    tongues,
  That most may claim this argument for ours?
DONALBAIN, ⌜*aside to Malcolm*⌝
  What should be spoken here, where our fate,
  Hid in an auger hole, may rush and seize us?
  Let's away. Our tears are not yet brewed.   145
MALCOLM, ⌜*aside to Donalbain*⌝
  Nor our strong sorrow upon the foot of motion.
BANQUO Look to the lady.
            ⌜*Lady Macbeth is assisted to leave.*⌝
  And when we have our naked frailties hid,
  That suffer in exposure, let us meet
  And question this most bloody piece of work   150
  To know it further. Fears and scruples shake us.
  In the great hand of God I stand, and thence
  Against the undivulged pretense I fight
  Of treasonous malice.
MACDUFF   And so do I.   155
ALL   So all.
MACBETH
  Let's briefly put on manly readiness
  And meet i' th' hall together.
ALL   Well contented.
            ⌜*All but Malcolm and Donalbain*⌝ *exit.*
MALCOLM
  What will you do? Let's not consort with them.   160
  To show an unfelt sorrow is an office
  Which the false man does easy. I'll to England.

165–66. **The near . . . bloody:** a common expression, reminiscent of Matthew 10.36: "a man's enemies shall be they of his own household" **near:** nearer

170. **dainty of:** polite about

171. **shift away:** go away stealthily

2.4 An old man and Ross exchange accounts of recent unnatural happenings. Macduff joins them to report that Malcolm and Donalbain are now accused of having bribed the servants who supposedly killed Duncan. Macduff also announces that Macbeth has been chosen king. Ross leaves for Scone and Macbeth's coronation, but Macduff resolves to stay at his own castle at Fife.

1. **Threescore and ten:** seventy years
3. **sore:** dreadful
5. **trifled former knowings:** made my earlier experiences seem trivial
8. **his bloody stage:** i.e., the Earth, on which man performs his bloody acts
10–12. **Is 't night's . . . kiss it?:** i.e., is it dark because night has become more powerful than day, or because day is hiding its face in shame?
15. **tow'ring in her pride of place:** circling at the top of her ascent (For picture of **falcon,** see page 74.)
16. **by a mousing owl hawked at:** attacked on the wing **by** an **owl,** whose normal prey is mice

DONALBAIN
  To Ireland I. Our separated fortune
  Shall keep us both the safer. Where we are,
  There's daggers in men's smiles. The near in blood, 165
  The nearer bloody.
MALCOLM   This murderous shaft that's shot
  Hath not yet lighted, and our safest way
  Is to avoid the aim. Therefore to horse,
  And let us not be dainty of leave-taking 170
  But shift away. There's warrant in that theft
  Which steals itself when there's no mercy left.
                                    They exit.

                    Scene 4

        Enter Ross with an Old Man.

OLD MAN
  Threescore and ten I can remember well,
  Within the volume of which time I have seen
  Hours dreadful and things strange, but this sore
     night
  Hath trifled former knowings. 5
ROSS   Ha, good father,
  Thou seest the heavens, as troubled with man's act,
  Threatens his bloody stage. By th' clock 'tis day,
  And yet dark night strangles the traveling lamp.
  Is 't night's predominance or the day's shame 10
  That darkness does the face of earth entomb
  When living light should kiss it?
OLD MAN   'Tis unnatural,
  Even like the deed that's done. On Tuesday last
  A falcon, tow'ring in her pride of place, 15
  Was by a mousing owl hawked at and killed.
ROSS
  And Duncan's horses (a thing most strange and
     certain),

19. **minions of their race:** choicest examples of their breed
21. **as: as** if
23. **eat:** ate
34. **good:** i.e., benefit (for themselves); **pretend:** intend
35. **suborned:** secretly bribed
40. **Thriftless:** unprofitable; **ravin up:** devour hungrily
43. **Scone:** the ancient royal city where Scottish kings were crowned
44. **invested:** (1) dressed in his coronation robes; (2) crowned
46. **Colmekill:** the small island (now called Iona), off the coast of Scotland, where Scottish kings were buried
47. **storehouse:** i.e., crypt, where the bodies were placed

A falcon. (2.4.15)
From George Turberville, *The booke of faulconrie* ... (1575).

Beauteous and swift, the minions of their race,
Turned wild in nature, broke their stalls, flung out, 20
Contending 'gainst obedience, as they would
Make war with mankind.
OLD MAN   'Tis said they eat each
  other.
ROSS
  They did so, to th' amazement of mine eyes 25
  That looked upon 't.

Enter Macduff.

                    Here comes the good
  Macduff.—
How goes the world, sir, now?
MACDUFF   Why, see you not? 30
ROSS
  Is 't known who did this more than bloody deed?
MACDUFF
  Those that Macbeth hath slain.
ROSS   Alas the day,
  What good could they pretend?
MACDUFF   They were suborned. 35
  Malcolm and Donalbain, the King's two sons,
  Are stol'n away and fled, which puts upon them
  Suspicion of the deed.
ROSS   'Gainst nature still!
  Thriftless ambition, that will ravin up 40
  Thine own lives' means. Then 'tis most like
  The sovereignty will fall upon Macbeth.
MACDUFF
  He is already named and gone to Scone
  To be invested.
ROSS   Where is Duncan's body? 45
MACDUFF   Carried to Colmekill,
  The sacred storehouse of his predecessors
  And guardian of their bones.

50. **Fife:** Macduff's castle
51. **thither:** i.e., to Scone
54. **father:** a term of respect for an elderly man
55. **benison:** blessing

Coronation of a Scottish king. (2.4.43–44)
From Raphael Holinshed, *The historie of Scotland* (1577).

ROSS   Will you to Scone?
MACDUFF
  No, cousin, I'll to Fife.   50
ROSS   Well, I will thither.
MACDUFF
  Well, may you see things well done there. Adieu,
  Lest our old robes sit easier than our new.
ROSS   Farewell, father.
OLD MAN
  God's benison go with you and with those   55
  That would make good of bad and friends of foes.
                                              All exit.

The Tragedy of
MACBETH

ACT 3

3.1 Banquo suspects that Macbeth killed Duncan in order to become king. Macbeth invites Banquo to a feast that night. Banquo promises to return in time. Macbeth, fearing that Banquo's children, not his own, will be the future kings of Scotland, seizes upon the opportunity provided by Banquo's scheduled return after dark to arrange for his murder. To carry out the crime, Macbeth employs two men whom he has persuaded to regard Banquo as an enemy.

---

    4. **stand:** be valid, hold good
    8. **by:** judging **by; on thee made good:** made **good** with regard to you
    10 SD. **Sennet:** flourish of trumpets to announce the entrance of a person of high degree
    13. **It had:** it would have; **as:** like
    14. **all-thing:** wholly
    15. **solemn:** ceremonial

ACT 3

Scene 1

Enter Banquo.

BANQUO
  Thou hast it now—king, Cawdor, Glamis, all
  As the Weïrd Women promised, and I fear
  Thou played'st most foully for 't. Yet it was said
  It should not stand in thy posterity,
  But that myself should be the root and father   5
  Of many kings. If there come truth from them
  (As upon thee, Macbeth, their speeches shine)
  Why, by the verities on thee made good,
  May they not be my oracles as well,
  And set me up in hope? But hush, no more.   10

  Sennet sounded. Enter Macbeth as King, Lady
  ⌜*Macbeth,*⌝ *Lennox, Ross, Lords, and Attendants.*

MACBETH
  Here's our chief guest.
LADY MACBETH   If he had been forgotten,
  It had been as a gap in our great feast
  And all-thing unbecoming.
MACBETH
  Tonight we hold a solemn supper, sir,
  And I'll request your presence.   15
BANQUO   Let your Highness

18. **Command upon me:** i.e., royally invite me (as opposed to **request,** line 16); **the which:** i.e., your commands; **duties:** obligations

24. **still:** always; **prosperous:** conducive to success

29–30. **I . . . twain:** i.e., **I must** ride an **hour** or two after dark

33. **bloody:** bloodthirsty; **cousins:** Malcolm and Donalbain

36. **invention:** fictions

37. **therewithal:** in addition to that; **cause of state:** state affairs

38. **Craving us jointly:** requiring the attention of both of us; **Hie:** hurry

45. **society:** (your) companionship

46. **The sweeter welcome:** the more sweetly welcome (to me)

46–47. **we will . . . alone:** I will stay . . . **alone**

47. **While then, God be with you:** until **then,** good-bye

Command upon me, to the which my duties
Are with a most indissoluble tie
Forever knit.
MACBETH   Ride you this afternoon?
BANQUO   Ay, my good lord.
MACBETH
We should have else desired your good advice
(Which still hath been both grave and prosperous)
In this day's council, but we'll take tomorrow.
Is 't far you ride?
BANQUO
As far, my lord, as will fill up the time
'Twixt this and supper. Go not my horse the better,
I must become a borrower of the night
For a dark hour or twain.
MACBETH   Fail not our feast.
BANQUO   My lord, I will not.
MACBETH
We hear our bloody cousins are bestowed
In England and in Ireland, not confessing
Their cruel parricide, filling their hearers
With strange invention. But of that tomorrow,
When therewithal we shall have cause of state
Craving us jointly. Hie you to horse. Adieu,
Till you return at night. Goes Fleance with you?
BANQUO
Ay, my good lord. Our time does call upon 's.
MACBETH
I wish your horses swift and sure of foot,
And so I do commend you to their backs.
Farewell.   *Banquo exits.*
Let every man be master of his time
Till seven at night. To make society
The sweeter welcome, we will keep ourself
Till suppertime alone. While then, God be with you.
    Lords ⌐and all but Macbeth and a Servant⌐ exit.

48. **Sirrah:** term of address to a social inferior
48–49. **Attend . . . pleasure:** i.e., are **those men** waiting to see me?
50. **without:** outside
55. **would be:** ought to **be**
57. **to:** in addition to
61. **genius:** attendant spirit; **rebuked:** checked
62. **Caesar:** i.e., Octavius **Caesar** (Shakespeare will write about this again in *Antony and Cleopatra*.)
66. **fruitless:** without offspring
69. **succeeding:** inheriting the kingship
70. **issue:** descendants; **filed:** made foul, defiled
72. **rancors:** bitter ill-feelings
73. **eternal jewel:** i.e., soul
74. **common enemy:** i.e., the devil **common:** general
75. **seeds:** sons
76. **come fate:** let **fate come; list:** lists, arena for trial by combat
77. **champion me:** oppose me; **to th' utterance:** to the death (*à l'outrance*, "to the uttermost, to extremity")
77 SD. **Murderers:** i.e., men whom Macbeth will persuade to commit murder (See longer note, page 194.)

Sirrah, a word with you. Attend those men
Our pleasure?
SERVANT
They are, my lord, without the palace gate.   50
MACBETH
Bring them before us.   *Servant exits.*
            To be thus is nothing,
But to be safely thus. Our fears in Banquo
Stick deep, and in his royalty of nature
Reigns that which would be feared. 'Tis much he   55
  dares,
And to that dauntless temper of his mind
He hath a wisdom that doth guide his valor
To act in safety. There is none but he
Whose being I do fear; and under him   60
My genius is rebuked, as it is said
Mark Antony's was by Caesar. He chid the sisters
When first they put the name of king upon me
And bade them speak to him. Then, prophet-like,
They hailed him father to a line of kings.   65
Upon my head they placed a fruitless crown
And put a barren scepter in my grip,
Thence to be wrenched with an unlineal hand,
No son of mine succeeding. If 't be so,
For Banquo's issue have I filed my mind;   70
For them the gracious Duncan have I murdered,
Put rancors in the vessel of my peace
Only for them, and mine eternal jewel
Given to the common enemy of man
To make them kings, the seeds of Banquo kings.   75
Rather than so, come fate into the list,
And champion me to th' utterance.—Who's there?

          Enter Servant and two Murderers.

⌜*To the Servant.*⌝ Now go to the door, and stay there
   till we call.   *Servant exits.*

87. **in probation:** in proving it

88. **borne in hand:** deceived, deluded (from the French *maintenir*); **crossed:** thwarted; also barred, debarred, shut out

89. **instruments:** means; also legal **instruments** such as were often used to strip men of their property

92. **To half a soul:** i.e., even to a half-wit; **a notion:** an understanding, a mind

98. **gospeled:** ruled by the Gospels' "love your enemies"

101. **yours:** your descendants

103. **catalogue:** list (of human types); **go for:** i.e., are counted as

106. **Shoughs:** rough-haired lapdogs; **water-rugs:** perhaps, water spaniels (See picture, below.) **demi-wolves:** crossbreeds of dog and wolf; **clept:** called

107. **valued file:** a list that evaluates each breed

109. **housekeeper:** watchdog

111. **closed:** enclosed

A water-rug, or water spaniel. (3.1.106)
From Edward Topsell, *The historie of foure-footed beastes* . . . (1607).

Was it not yesterday we spoke together? 80
⌜MURDERERS⌝
It was, so please your Highness.
MACBETH   Well then, now
Have you considered of my speeches? Know
That it was he, in the times past, which held you
So under fortune, which you thought had been 85
Our innocent self. This I made good to you
In our last conference, passed in probation with you
How you were borne in hand, how crossed, the
  instruments,
Who wrought with them, and all things else that 90
  might
To half a soul and to a notion crazed
Say "Thus did Banquo."
FIRST MURDERER   You made it known to us.
MACBETH
I did so, and went further, which is now 95
Our point of second meeting. Do you find
Your patience so predominant in your nature
That you can let this go? Are you so gospeled
To pray for this good man and for his issue,
Whose heavy hand hath bowed you to the grave 100
And beggared yours forever?
FIRST MURDERER   We are men, my liege.
MACBETH
Ay, in the catalogue you go for men,
As hounds and greyhounds, mongrels, spaniels,
  curs, 105
Shoughs, water-rugs, and demi-wolves are clept
All by the name of dogs. The valued file
Distinguishes the swift, the slow, the subtle,
The housekeeper, the hunter, every one
According to the gift which bounteous nature 110
Hath in him closed; whereby he does receive

112. **Particular addition:** a special name or title

112–13. **from the bill . . . alike:** in distinction **from the** catalogue that simply lists them all as *dogs*

114. **station:** position; **file:** wordplay on **file** as "list" (line 107) and as a "row of soldiers lined up one behind the other"

115. **rank:** wordplay on **rank** as "relative position" and as a "row of soldiers lined up abreast"

116. **in your bosoms:** into your care

117. **Whose execution:** the carrying out of which; **takes . . . off:** gets rid of **your enemy**

119. **in his life:** because Banquo is alive

120. **were perfect:** would be completely contented

126. **tugged with:** pulled about by

127. **set:** stake, venture; **chance:** eventuality

128. **on 't:** of it

132. **bloody:** portending bloodshed; **distance:** hostility, discord (**Distance** is also a technical term in fencing. The image thus suggested of the two in a potentially fatal duel is sustained in the word **thrusts,** line 133.)

134. **my near'st of life:** i.e., (1) the part most essential to **life**—the heart; (2) my most vital spot

136. **bid my will avouch it:** offer my desire for Banquo's death as sufficient justification for killing him

137. **For:** because of

138. **but wail:** i.e., but I must, instead, bewail

140. **to . . . make love:** court your help

Particular addition, from the bill
That writes them all alike. And so of men.
Now, if you have a station in the file,
Not i' th' worst rank of manhood, say 't, 115
And I will put that business in your bosoms
Whose execution takes your enemy off,
Grapples you to the heart and love of us,
Who wear our health but sickly in his life,
Which in his death were perfect. 120
SECOND MURDERER　　　　　　I am one, my liege,
Whom the vile blows and buffets of the world
Hath so incensed that I am reckless what
I do to spite the world.
FIRST MURDERER　　　And I another 125
So weary with disasters, tugged with fortune,
That I would set my life on any chance,
To mend it or be rid on 't.
MACBETH　　　　　　　Both of you
Know Banquo was your enemy. 130
⌜MURDERERS⌝　　　　　　True, my lord.
MACBETH
So is he mine, and in such bloody distance
That every minute of his being thrusts
Against my near'st of life. And though I could
With barefaced power sweep him from my sight 135
And bid my will avouch it, yet I must not,
For certain friends that are both his and mine,
Whose loves I may not drop, but wail his fall
Who I myself struck down. And thence it is
That I to your assistance do make love, 140
Masking the business from the common eye
For sundry weighty reasons.
SECOND MURDERER　　　　We shall, my lord,
Perform what you command us.
FIRST MURDERER　　　　　　Though our lives— 145

146. **spirits:** courage, vital powers
149. **perfect spy o' th' time:** perhaps, exact information about when the deed should be done (This puzzling line has no agreed-upon meaning.)
150. **on 't:** of it
151. **something from:** somewhat away from; **always thought:** it being **always** understood
152. **I require a clearness:** I must be kept clear
153. **rubs nor botches:** flaws or defects
155. **absence:** i.e., removal, death; **material:** important
157. **Resolve yourselves apart:** make up your minds in private
160. **straight:** straightway, immediately
161. **concluded:** settled, determined

3.2 Both Lady Macbeth and Macbeth express their unhappiness. Macbeth speaks of his fear of Banquo especially. He refers to a dreadful deed that will happen that night but does not confide his plan for Banquo's murder to Lady Macbeth.

---

3. **attend his leisure:** The phrase "**attend** someone's **leisure**" means to wait until he or she is unoccupied.
6. **spent:** used up, exhausted
9. **doubtful:** apprehensive

MACBETH
  Your spirits shine through you. Within this hour at
    most
  I will advise you where to plant yourselves,
  Acquaint you with the perfect spy o' th' time,
  The moment on 't, for 't must be done tonight   150
  And something from the palace; always thought
  That I require a clearness. And with him
  (To leave no rubs nor botches in the work)
  Fleance, his son, that keeps him company,
  Whose absence is no less material to me   155
  Than is his father's, must embrace the fate
  Of that dark hour. Resolve yourselves apart.
  I'll come to you anon.
⌜MURDERERS⌝ We are resolved, my lord.
MACBETH
  I'll call upon you straight. Abide within.   160
                              ⌜*Murderers exit.*⌝
  It is concluded. Banquo, thy soul's flight,
  If it find heaven, must find it out tonight.
                              ⌜*He exits.*⌝

                     Scene 2

         Enter Macbeth's Lady and a Servant.

LADY MACBETH Is Banquo gone from court?
SERVANT
  Ay, madam, but returns again tonight.
LADY MACBETH
  Say to the King I would attend his leisure
  For a few words.
SERVANT Madam, I will.   *He exits.*   5
LADY MACBETH Naught's had, all's spent,
  Where our desire is got without content.
  'Tis safer to be that which we destroy
  Than by destruction dwell in doubtful joy.

11. **sorriest:** most wretched
12. **Using:** entertaining, harboring
13. **without:** beyond; **all:** any
15. **scorched:** slashed (from *score*, to slash as with a knife)
16. **close:** come back together, heal
16–17. **our poor malice / Remains:** i.e., I, who have committed a malicious act (which now seems weak and ineffective), remain (**Our** may be instead a simple plural, though elsewhere in the speech—e.g., lines 18–22—Macbeth clearly uses the royal plural.) **poor:** weak, ineffective   **malice:** malicious act
17. **her former tooth:** i.e., the snake's **tooth** (**her** poisoned fang) as it was before she was **scorched**
18. **frame:** structure; **disjoint:** come apart
18–19. **both the worlds suffer:** (let) heaven and Earth perish
25. **In restless ecstasy:** in a frenzy of sleeplessness
27. **his:** its; **nor . . . nor:** neither . . . nor
28. **Malice domestic:** civil ill will; **foreign levy:** armies from abroad
30. **gentle my lord:** my noble **lord**
31. **Sleek o'er:** smooth over; **rugged looks:** i.e., furrowed brows
35–36. **present . . . tongue:** give him special honor by look and speech
36. **unsafe the while that:** (you and I) are **unsafe** during this time in which
37. **lave our honors:** wash our reputations
38. **vizards:** masks, visors
40. **leave this:** stop talking and thinking this way

Enter Macbeth.

How now, my lord, why do you keep alone, 10
Of sorriest fancies your companions making,
Using those thoughts which should indeed have died
With them they think on? Things without all remedy
Should be without regard. What's done is done.

MACBETH
We have scorched the snake, not killed it. 15
She'll close and be herself whilst our poor malice
Remains in danger of her former tooth.
But let the frame of things disjoint, both the worlds suffer,
Ere we will eat our meal in fear, and sleep 20
In the affliction of these terrible dreams
That shake us nightly. Better be with the dead,
Whom we, to gain our peace, have sent to peace,
Than on the torture of the mind to lie
In restless ecstasy. Duncan is in his grave. 25
After life's fitful fever he sleeps well.
Treason has done his worst; nor steel nor poison,
Malice domestic, foreign levy, nothing
Can touch him further.

LADY MACBETH   Come on, gentle my lord, 30
Sleek o'er your rugged looks. Be bright and jovial
Among your guests tonight.

MACBETH   So shall I, love,
And so I pray be you. Let your remembrance
Apply to Banquo; present him eminence 35
Both with eye and tongue: unsafe the while that we
Must lave our honors in these flattering streams
And make our faces vizards to our hearts,
Disguising what they are.

LADY MACBETH   You must leave this. 40

MACBETH
O, full of scorpions is my mind, dear wife!
Thou know'st that Banquo and his Fleance lives.

43. **nature's copy's not eterne:** i.e., they have not been granted eternal life   **copy:** perhaps, copyhold tenure (a lease held by the lord of the manor); or, the individual copied from **nature's** mold

45–46. **flown . . . flight:** i.e., emerged (at twilight) from the secluded caves and dark corners where bats sleep during the day

46. **Hecate:** a powerful goddess and the patron of witches

47. **shard-born:** born in dung (See longer note, page 195.)

48. **rung night's yawning peal:** i.e., finished announcing, with its **hums,** the coming of sleepy night (The image is of the pealing of the curfew bell.)

52. **seeling night:** i.e., **night** that blinds the eyes (The image is of the sewing together of the eyelids of the falcon to keep it temporarily in darkness.)

53. **Scarf up:** blindfold; **pitiful:** compassionate

55. **Cancel . . . bond:** i.e., remove Banquo and Fleance (See longer note, page 195.)

57. **rooky:** i.e., filled with rooks

3.3 A third man joins the two whom Macbeth has already sent to kill Banquo and Fleance. The three assassins manage to kill Banquo. Fleance escapes.

3. **He:** i.e., the third murderer; **delivers:** reports
4. **offices:** duties
5. **To the direction just:** exactly according to (our) instructions (from Macbeth)

LADY MACBETH
  But in them nature's copy's not eterne.
MACBETH
  There's comfort yet; they are assailable.
  Then be thou jocund. Ere the bat hath flown   45
  His cloistered flight, ere to black Hecate's summons
  The shard-born beetle with his drowsy hums
  Hath rung night's yawning peal, there shall be done
  A deed of dreadful note.
LADY MACBETH   What's to be done?   50
MACBETH
  Be innocent of the knowledge, dearest chuck,
  Till thou applaud the deed.—Come, seeling night,
  Scarf up the tender eye of pitiful day
  And with thy bloody and invisible hand
  Cancel and tear to pieces that great bond   55
  Which keeps me pale. Light thickens, and the crow
  Makes wing to th' rooky wood.
  Good things of day begin to droop and drowse,
  Whiles night's black agents to their preys do
    rouse.—   60
  Thou marvel'st at my words, but hold thee still.
  Things bad begun make strong themselves by ill.
  So prithee go with me.
                                    They exit.

Scene 3

Enter three Murderers.

FIRST MURDERER
  But who did bid thee join with us?
THIRD MURDERER   Macbeth.
SECOND MURDERER, ⌜*to the First Murderer*⌝
  He needs not our mistrust, since he delivers
  Our offices and what we have to do
  To the direction just.   5

8. **lated:** belated, tardy
9. **timely:** opportune, welcome
10. **The subject of our watch:** the person we are waiting for
12 SD. **within:** offstage
14. **within the note of expectation:** i.e., included in the list of expected guests
16. **go about:** perhaps, are being led to the stables or away from the **palace gate** (line 18)

A Scottish thane killed in ambush. (3.3.24–26)
From Raphael Holinshed, *The historie of Scotland* (1577).

FIRST MURDERER   Then stand with us.—
  The west yet glimmers with some streaks of day.
  Now spurs the lated traveler apace
  To gain the timely inn, ⌜and⌝ near approaches
  The subject of our watch.
THIRD MURDERER   Hark, I hear horses.
BANQUO, *within*   Give us a light there, ho!
SECOND MURDERER   Then 'tis he. The rest
  That are within the note of expectation
  Already are i' th' court.
FIRST MURDERER   His horses go about.
THIRD MURDERER
  Almost a mile; but he does usually
  (So all men do) from hence to th' palace gate
  Make it their walk.

  Enter Banquo and Fleance, with a torch.

SECOND MURDERER   A light, a light!
THIRD MURDERER   'Tis he.
FIRST MURDERER   Stand to 't.
BANQUO, ⌜*to Fleance*⌝   It will be rain tonight.
FIRST MURDERER   Let it come down!
                    ⌜*The three Murderers attack.*⌝
BANQUO
  O treachery! Fly, good Fleance, fly, fly, fly!
  Thou mayst revenge—O slave!
                    ⌜*He dies. Fleance exits.*⌝
THIRD MURDERER
  Who did strike out the light?
FIRST MURDERER   Was 't not the way?
THIRD MURDERER   There's but one down. The son is
  fled.
SECOND MURDERER   We have lost best half of our
  affair.
FIRST MURDERER
  Well, let's away and say how much is done.
                    They exit.

3.4 As Macbeth's banquet begins, one of Banquo's murderers appears at the door to tell Macbeth of Banquo's death and Fleance's escape. Returning to the table, Macbeth is confronted by Banquo's ghost, invisible to all but Macbeth. While Lady Macbeth is able to dismiss as a momentary fit Macbeth's expressions of horror at the ghost's first appearance, the reappearance of the ghost and Macbeth's outcries in response to it force Lady Macbeth to send all the guests away. Alone with Lady Macbeth, Macbeth resolves to meet the witches again. He foresees a future marked by further violence.

---

1. **degrees:** relative status (and hence where you are entitled to sit)
1–2. **At first / And last:** to all in whatever degree
6. **keeps her state:** remains on her throne; **in best time:** at the most proper moment
7. **require:** request
10. **encounter thee:** respond to your welcome (perhaps with low bows as they take their places)
11. **Both sides are even:** perhaps, there are equal numbers on **both sides** of the table
12. **large:** liberal, unrestrained; **Anon:** soon; **measure:** i.e., a toast
21. **the nonpareil:** without equal
23. **I ... perfect: I** otherwise would have **been** fully secure, complete

Scene 4

*Banquet prepared. Enter Macbeth, Lady ⌐Macbeth,¬
Ross, Lennox, Lords, and Attendants.*

MACBETH
You know your own degrees; sit down. At first
And last, the hearty welcome.   ⌐*They sit.*¬
LORDS   Thanks to your Majesty.
MACBETH
Ourself will mingle with society
And play the humble host.   5
Our hostess keeps her state, but in best time
We will require her welcome.
LADY MACBETH
Pronounce it for me, sir, to all our friends,
For my heart speaks they are welcome.

Enter First Murderer ⌐to the door.¬

MACBETH
See, they encounter thee with their hearts' thanks.   10
Both sides are even. Here I'll sit i' th' midst.
Be large in mirth. Anon we'll drink a measure
The table round. ⌐*Approaching the Murderer.*¬ There's
    blood upon thy face.
MURDERER   'Tis Banquo's then.   15
MACBETH
'Tis better thee without than he within.
Is he dispatched?
MURDERER
My lord, his throat is cut. That I did for him.
MACBETH
Thou art the best o' th' cutthroats,
Yet he's good that did the like for Fleance.   20
If thou didst it, thou art the nonpareil.
MURDERER
Most royal sir, Fleance is 'scaped.
MACBETH, ⌐*aside*¬
Then comes my fit again. I had else been perfect,

24. **founded:** rooted, stable
25. **broad:** free; **casing:** surrounding, enclosing
26. **cabined, cribbed:** closed in, cramped (as in a cabin or hovel)
27. **saucy:** insolent; **safe:** unable to do harm
28. **bides:** remains; waits
30. **The least a death to nature:** the smallest one of which would have been fatal
32. **worm:** i.e., young serpent
35. **hear ourselves:** talk
37. **give the cheer:** i.e., entertain your guests properly; **sold:** i.e., as opposed to **given** (line 39), as if the host were an innkeeper (Lines 37–39 say that a feast is no better than a meal in an inn if the host does not keep assuring his guests of their welcome.)
39. **To feed ... home:** mere eating is best done **at home**
40. **From thence:** i.e., (when one is) away from home; **meat:** food; **ceremony:** the practice of courtesy
41. **Meeting were:** social gatherings would be
41 SD. **Enter the Ghost:** The ghost is not observed by Macbeth until line 54. (See longer note, page 196.)
43. **wait on:** serve, and therefore follow upon
46. **our country's honor roofed:** i.e., all the nobility of the country under one roof
48–49. **Who ... mischance:** whom I hope I should blame for unkindly staying away rather than pity for some accident that has happened to him
51. **Lays ... promise:** i.e., calls into question **his promise** (to be here)

Whole as the marble, founded as the rock,
As broad and general as the casing air.
But now I am cabined, cribbed, confined, bound in
To saucy doubts and fears.—But Banquo's safe?
MURDERER
Ay, my good lord. Safe in a ditch he bides,
With twenty trenchèd gashes on his head,
The least a death to nature.
MACBETH   Thanks for that.
There the grown serpent lies. The worm that's fled
Hath nature that in time will venom breed,
No teeth for th' present. Get thee gone. Tomorrow
We'll hear ourselves again.   *Murderer exits.*
LADY MACBETH   My royal lord,
You do not give the cheer. The feast is sold
That is not often vouched, while 'tis a-making,
'Tis given with welcome. To feed were best at home;
From thence, the sauce to meat is ceremony;
Meeting were bare without it.

Enter the Ghost of Banquo, and sits in Macbeth's place.

MACBETH, ⌜*to Lady Macbeth*⌝ Sweet remembrancer!—
Now, good digestion wait on appetite
And health on both!
LENNOX   May 't please your Highness sit.
MACBETH
Here had we now our country's honor roofed,
Were the graced person of our Banquo present,
Who may I rather challenge for unkindness
Than pity for mischance.
ROSS   His absence, sir,
Lays blame upon his promise. Please 't your
    Highness
To grace us with your royal company?
MACBETH
The table's full.

57. **moves:** disturbs
66. **upon a thought:** in a moment
67. **note:** pay attention to
68. **passion:** disturbed state
75. **air-drawn:** made of air, airy
76. **flaws and starts:** outbursts
77. **to:** in comparison to; **well become:** be very appropriate for
78. **woman's story:** i.e., "old wives' tale" (See picture, below.)
79. **Authorized by:** vouched for, with a sense also of "authored by"; **Shame itself!:** i.e., for **shame**!

A woman "at a winter's fire." (3.4.78)
From Jacob Cats, *Alle de werken* ... (1657–59).

LENNOX   Here is a place reserved, sir.   55
MACBETH Where?
LENNOX
  Here, my good lord. What is 't that moves your
    Highness?
MACBETH
  Which of you have done this?
LORDS   What, my good lord?   60
MACBETH, ⌜*to the Ghost*⌝
  Thou canst not say I did it. Never shake
  Thy gory locks at me.
ROSS
  Gentlemen, rise. His Highness is not well.
LADY MACBETH
  Sit, worthy friends. My lord is often thus
  And hath been from his youth. Pray you, keep seat.   65
  The fit is momentary; upon a thought
  He will again be well. If much you note him,
  You shall offend him and extend his passion.
  Feed and regard him not. ⌜*Drawing Macbeth aside.*⌝
                       Are you a man?   70
MACBETH
  Ay, and a bold one, that dare look on that
  Which might appall the devil.
LADY MACBETH   O, proper stuff!
  This is the very painting of your fear.
  This is the air-drawn dagger which you said   75
  Led you to Duncan. O, these flaws and starts,
  Impostors to true fear, would well become
  A woman's story at a winter's fire,
  Authorized by her grandam. Shame itself!
  Why do you make such faces? When all's done,   80
  You look but on a stool.
MACBETH
  Prithee, see there. Behold, look! ⌜*To the Ghost.*⌝ Lo,
    how say you?

85. **charnel houses:** vaults or small buildings for the bones of the dead (See picture, below.)

86–87. **our monuments ... kites:** i.e., **our** only burial vaults (**monuments**) will be the stomachs (**maws**) of birds of prey (**kites**) See picture, page 106.

92. **humane:** civil, kindly; **purged the gentle weal:** cleansed the commonwealth of violence and made it **gentle**

97. **crowns:** heads

101. **lack you:** miss your company

107 SD. **Enter Ghost:** The ghost is not observed by Macbeth until line 113. See longer note on 3.4.41 SD.

110, **him we thirst: (to) him we** wish or long for (i.e., Banquo)

113. **Avaunt:** begone; **quit:** leave

A charnel house. (3.4.85)
From *Todten-Tantz* ... (1696).

Why, what care I? If thou canst nod, speak too.—
If charnel houses and our graves must send   85
Those that we bury back, our monuments
Shall be the maws of kites.   ⌜*Ghost exits.*⌝
LADY MACBETH   What, quite unmanned in folly?
MACBETH
  If I stand here, I saw him.
LADY MACBETH   Fie, for shame!   90
MACBETH
  Blood hath been shed ere now, i' th' olden time,
  Ere humane statute purged the gentle weal;
  Ay, and since too, murders have been performed
  Too terrible for the ear. The ⌜time⌝ has been
  That, when the brains were out, the man would die,   95
  And there an end. But now they rise again
  With twenty mortal murders on their crowns
  And push us from our stools. This is more strange
  Than such a murder is.
LADY MACBETH   My worthy lord,   100
  Your noble friends do lack you.
MACBETH   I do forget.—
  Do not muse at me, my most worthy friends.
  I have a strange infirmity, which is nothing
  To those that know me. Come, love and health to   105
     all.
  Then I'll sit down.—Give me some wine. Fill full.

            Enter Ghost.

  I drink to th' general joy o' th' whole table
  And to our dear friend Banquo, whom we miss.
  Would he were here! To all, and him we thirst,   110
  And all to all.
LORDS   Our duties, and the pledge.
            ⌜*They raise their drinking cups.*⌝
MACBETH, ⌜*to the Ghost*⌝
  Avaunt, and quit my sight! Let the earth hide thee.
  Thy bones are marrowless; thy blood is cold;

115. **speculation:** ability to see
119. **a thing of custom:** something customary
123. **Hyrcan:** from Hyrcania, a part of the Roman Empire located on the Caspian Sea (In the *Aeneid*, Hyrcania is associated with tigers.)
124. **nerves:** sinews
126. **desert:** (any) uninhabited place
127. **If trembling I inhabit then:** perhaps, if **I then** tremble; **protest me:** proclaim me
128. **The baby of a girl:** i.e., a baby **girl**
129. **mock'ry:** illusion (with perhaps the sense, also, of "that which mocks me")
130. **being gone:** i.e., it **being gone**
134. **admired:** amazing
137–38. **strange . . . owe:** i.e., feel like a stranger to my own nature   **owe:** own
146. **Stand not . . . going:** i.e., don't insist on leaving in ceremonial rank **order**

A kite. (3.4.87; 4.3.256)
From Konrad Gesner, . . . *Historiae animalium* . . . (1585–1604).

Thou hast no speculation in those eyes 115
Which thou dost glare with.
LADY MACBETH   Think of this, good
  peers,
But as a thing of custom. 'Tis no other;
Only it spoils the pleasure of the time. 120
MACBETH, ⌜*to the Ghost*⌝   What man dare, I dare.
Approach thou like the rugged Russian bear,
The armed rhinoceros, or th' Hyrcan tiger;
Take any shape but that, and my firm nerves
Shall never tremble. Or be alive again 125
And dare me to the desert with thy sword.
If trembling I inhabit then, protest me
The baby of a girl. Hence, horrible shadow!
Unreal mock'ry, hence!   ⌜*Ghost exits.*⌝
                  Why so, being gone, 130
I am a man again.—Pray you sit still.
LADY MACBETH
You have displaced the mirth, broke the good
  meeting
With most admired disorder.
MACBETH   Can such things be 135
And overcome us like a summer's cloud,
Without our special wonder? You make me strange
Even to the disposition that I owe
When now I think you can behold such sights
And keep the natural ruby of your cheeks 140
When mine is blanched with fear.
ROSS   What sights, my
  lord?
LADY MACBETH
I pray you, speak not. He grows worse and worse.
Question enrages him. At once, good night. 145
Stand not upon the order of your going,
But go at once.
LENNOX   Good night, and better health
Attend his Majesty.

154. **Augurs:** i.e., auguries, predictions; **understood relations:** comprehended reports

155. **By maggot pies and choughs:** i.e., by means of magpies and jackdaws

155–56. **brought forth:** revealed

157. **man of blood:** murderer; **What is the night?:** what time of **night is** it?

164. **fee'd:** paid (to spy)

165. **betimes:** early

166. **bent:** determined

169. **no more: no** further

171. **will to hand:** demand to be carried out

172. **scanned:** thought about carefully

173. **season:** seasoning (i.e., that which preserves and gives flavor or zest)

174. **strange and self-abuse:** remarkable self-delusion

175. **initiate fear:** i.e., **fear** felt by a beginner, an initiate; **wants:** lacks, needs; **hard use:** practice that hardens one; or, vigorous usage

LADY MACBETH A kind good night to all.
  Lords ⌈and all but Macbeth and Lady Macbeth⌉ exit.
MACBETH
  It will have blood, they say; blood will have blood.
  Stones have been known to move, and trees to
    speak.
  Augurs and understood relations have
  By maggot pies and choughs and rooks brought
    forth
  The secret'st man of blood.—What is the night?
LADY MACBETH
  Almost at odds with morning, which is which.
MACBETH
  How say'st thou that Macduff denies his person
  At our great bidding?
LADY MACBETH   Did you send to him, sir?
MACBETH
  I hear it by the way; but I will send.
  There's not a one of them but in his house
  I keep a servant fee'd. I will tomorrow
  (And betimes I will) to the Weïrd Sisters.
  More shall they speak, for now I am bent to know
  By the worst means the worst. For mine own good,
  All causes shall give way. I am in blood
  Stepped in so far that, should I wade no more,
  Returning were as tedious as go o'er.
  Strange things I have in head that will to hand,
  Which must be acted ere they may be scanned.
LADY MACBETH
  You lack the season of all natures, sleep.
MACBETH
  Come, we'll to sleep. My strange and self-abuse
  Is the initiate fear that wants hard use.
  We are yet but young in deed.
                              They exit.

3.5 The presentation of the witches in this scene (as in 4.1.38 SD–43 and 141–48) differs from their presentation in the rest of the play. Most editors and scholars believe that neither this scene nor the passages in 4.1 were written by Shakespeare.

---

   2. **beldams:** hags
   7. **close:** secret
  15. **Acheron:** a river in the underworld, in Greek mythology
  24. **profound:** of deep significance
  27. **artificial:** deceitful; skilled in artifice
  29. **confusion:** destruction

Fortune turning mortals on her wheel. (3.1.126–28)
From Gregor Reisch, *Margarita philosophica* . . . (1503).

Scene 5

Thunder. Enter the three Witches, meeting Hecate.

FIRST WITCH
  Why, how now, Hecate? You look angerly.
HECATE
  Have I not reason, beldams as you are?
  Saucy and overbold, how did you dare
  To trade and traffic with Macbeth
  In riddles and affairs of death, 5
  And I, the mistress of your charms,
  The close contriver of all harms,
  Was never called to bear my part
  Or show the glory of our art?
  And which is worse, all you have done 10
  Hath been but for a wayward son,
  Spiteful and wrathful, who, as others do,
  Loves for his own ends, not for you.
  But make amends now. Get you gone,
  And at the pit of Acheron 15
  Meet me i' th' morning. Thither he
  Will come to know his destiny.
  Your vessels and your spells provide,
  Your charms and everything beside.
  I am for th' air. This night I'll spend 20
  Unto a dismal and a fatal end.
  Great business must be wrought ere noon.
  Upon the corner of the moon
  There hangs a vap'rous drop profound.
  I'll catch it ere it come to ground, 25
  And that, distilled by magic sleights,
  Shall raise such artificial sprites
  As by the strength of their illusion
  Shall draw him on to his confusion.
  He shall spurn fate, scorn death, and bear 30
  His hopes 'bove wisdom, grace, and fear.

32. **security:** too much self-confidence
35 SD. **Come away:** This song is from Thomas Middleton's play *The Witch* (Act 3, scene 3). The first two lines read "Come away! Come away! / Hecate, Hecate, come away!" Most scholars think that *Macbeth* 3.5, as well as parts of 4.1, were written by Middleton, perhaps for a revival of the play later in James's reign. Some attribute even more of the play to Middleton.

3.6 Lennox and an unnamed lord discuss politics in Scotland. Lennox comments sarcastically upon Macbeth's "official" versions of the many recent violent deaths. The nameless lord responds with news of Macduff's flight to England to seek help in overthrowing Macbeth.

---

1. **but hit your thoughts:** merely agreed with what you were already thinking
2. **interpret farther:** i.e., go on to draw further conclusions
3. **borne:** managed, conducted
5. **of:** by; **marry:** a mild oath (originally an oath on the name of Mary, mother of Jesus)
9. **want the thought:** help thinking
11. **fact:** deed, crime
12. **straight:** immediately
13. **delinquents:** offenders
14. **slaves of drink:** i.e., in a drunken stupor; **thralls:** slaves
20. **an 't:** if it

    And you all know, security
    Is mortals' chiefest enemy.
                           Music and a song.
    Hark! I am called. My little spirit, see,
    Sits in a foggy cloud and stays for me. ⌜*Hecate exits.*⌝   35
          Sing within "Come away, come away," etc.

FIRST WITCH
    Come, let's make haste. She'll soon be back again.
                                  They exit.

Scene 6

Enter Lennox and another Lord.

LENNOX
    My former speeches have but hit your thoughts,
    Which can interpret farther. Only I say
    Things have been strangely borne. The gracious
        Duncan
    Was pitied of Macbeth; marry, he was dead.   5
    And the right valiant Banquo walked too late,
    Whom you may say, if 't please you, Fleance killed,
    For Fleance fled. Men must not walk too late.
    Who cannot want the thought how monstrous
    It was for Malcolm and for Donalbain   10
    To kill their gracious father? Damnèd fact,
    How it did grieve Macbeth! Did he not straight
    In pious rage the two delinquents tear
    That were the slaves of drink and thralls of sleep?
    Was not that nobly done? Ay, and wisely, too,   15
    For 'twould have angered any heart alive
    To hear the men deny 't. So that I say
    He has borne all things well. And I do think
    That had he Duncan's sons under his key
    (As, an 't please heaven, he shall not) they should   20
        find
    What 'twere to kill a father. So should Fleance.

23. **from broad words:** as a result of plain speaking
28. **son of Duncan:** i.e., Malcolm
29. **holds:** withholds; **due of birth:** birthright
31. **Of:** by; **Edward: Edward** the Confessor, king of England from 1042 to 1066
32–33. **nothing / Takes:** does not detract
33. **his high respect:** the **high respect** granted Malcolm
34. **upon his aid:** on Malcolm's behalf
37. **ratify:** sanction
40. **free honors: honors** freely given
45. **an absolute . . . I:** i.e., Macduff had answered Macbeth's order to appear with a peremptory **"Sir, not I"**
46. **cloudy:** unhappy, gloomy; **turns me:** i.e., **turns**
48. **clogs:** burdens
50. **him:** i.e., Macduff
52. **unfold:** reveal
54–55. **our . . . accursed:** i.e., **our country, suffering under** an **accursed hand**

A hermit. (1.6.24)
From August Casimir Redel, *Apophtegmata symbolica* (n.d.).

 But peace. For from broad words, and 'cause he
  failed
 His presence at the tyrant's feast, I hear   25
 Macduff lives in disgrace. Sir, can you tell
 Where he bestows himself?
LORD   The ⌜son⌝ of Duncan
 (From whom this tyrant holds the due of birth)
 Lives in the English court and is received   30
 Of the most pious Edward with such grace
 That the malevolence of fortune nothing
 Takes from his high respect. Thither Macduff
 Is gone to pray the holy king upon his aid
 To wake Northumberland and warlike Siward 35
 That, by the help of these (with Him above
 To ratify the work), we may again
 Give to our tables meat, sleep to our nights,
 Free from our feasts and banquets bloody knives,
 Do faithful homage, and receive free honors, 40
 All which we pine for now. And this report
 Hath so exasperate ⌜the⌝ King that he
 Prepares for some attempt of war.
LENNOX Sent he to Macduff?
LORD
 He did, and with an absolute "Sir, not I,"   45
 The cloudy messenger turns me his back
 And hums, as who should say "You'll rue the time
 That clogs me with this answer."
LENNOX   And that well might
 Advise him to a caution ⌜t' hold⌝ what distance 50
 His wisdom can provide. Some holy angel
 Fly to the court of England and unfold
 His message ere he come, that a swift blessing
 May soon return to this our suffering country
 Under a hand accursed.   55
LORD I'll send my prayers with him.
              They exit.

The Tragedy of
MACBETH

ACT 4

4.1 Macbeth approaches the witches to learn how to make his kingship secure. In response they summon for him three apparitions: an armed head, a bloody child, and finally a child crowned, with a tree in his hand. These apparitions instruct Macbeth to beware Macduff but reassure him that no man born of woman can harm him and that he will not be overthrown until Birnam Wood moves to Dunsinane. Macbeth is greatly reassured, but his confidence in the future is shaken when the witches show him a line of kings all in the image of Banquo. After the witches disappear, Macbeth discovers that Macduff has fled to England and decides to kill Macduff's family immediately.

---

1. **brinded:** brindled, striped
2. **hedge-pig:** hedgehog
3. **Harpier:** perhaps the Third Witch's familiar

6–9. **Toad . . . pot:** i.e., first boil the **toad** that has sweated **venom** for **thirty-one days and nights under** a **cold stone**   **Sweltered:** exuded

12. **Fillet:** slice; **fenny:** i.e., living in a fen or swamp

ACT 4

Scene 1

Thunder. Enter the three Witches.

FIRST WITCH
  Thrice the brinded cat hath mewed.
SECOND WITCH
  Thrice, and once the hedge-pig whined.
THIRD WITCH
  Harpier cries "'Tis time, 'tis time!"
FIRST WITCH
  Round about the cauldron go;
  In the poisoned entrails throw.   5
  Toad, that under cold stone
  Days and nights has thirty-one
  Sweltered venom sleeping got,
  Boil thou first i' th' charmèd pot.
             ⌜*The Witches circle the cauldron.*⌝
ALL
  Double, double toil and trouble;   10
  Fire burn, and cauldron bubble.
SECOND WITCH
  Fillet of a fenny snake
  In the cauldron boil and bake.
  Eye of newt and toe of frog,
  Wool of bat and tongue of dog,   15
  Adder's fork and blindworm's sting,

119

17. **howlet:** owlet, small owl
23. **mummy:** mummified human flesh; **maw and gulf:** voracious belly
24. **ravined:** perhaps, ravenous; or, glutted
30. **birth-strangled:** i.e., killed as soon as born
31. **drab:** whore
32. **thick and slab:** viscous
33. **chaudron:** entrails
37. **baboon's:** accented on first syllable
39–43. **O . . . in:** These lines (and the stage direction preceding them) are thought by most scholars to be by another author. Since the song that the witches sing, "Black Spirits," is from Middleton's play *The Witch,* the lines may have been written by Middleton.

A baboon. (4.1.37)
From Edward Topsell, *The historie of foure-footed beastes* . . . (1607).

Lizard's leg and howlet's wing,
For a charm of powerful trouble,
Like a hell-broth boil and bubble.
ALL
Double, double toil and trouble;
Fire burn, and cauldron bubble.
THIRD WITCH
Scale of dragon, tooth of wolf,
Witch's mummy, maw and gulf
Of the ravined salt-sea shark,
Root of hemlock digged i' th' dark,
Liver of blaspheming Jew,
Gall of goat and slips of yew
Slivered in the moon's eclipse,
Nose of Turk and Tartar's lips,
Finger of birth-strangled babe
Ditch-delivered by a drab,
Make the gruel thick and slab.
Add thereto a tiger's chaudron
For th' ingredience of our cauldron.
ALL
Double, double toil and trouble;
Fire burn, and cauldron bubble.
SECOND WITCH
Cool it with a baboon's blood.
Then the charm is firm and good.

Enter Hecate ⌜to⌝ the other three Witches.

HECATE
O, well done! I commend your pains,
And everyone shall share i' th' gains.
And now about the cauldron sing
Like elves and fairies in a ring,
Enchanting all that you put in.
Music and a song: "Black Spirits," etc. ⌜*Hecate exits.*⌝

51. **conjure:** command, adjure
54. **yeasty:** foamy, frothy (See picture, below.)
55. **Confound:** destroy; **navigation:** i.e., ships
56. **bladed corn:** wheat not yet fully ripe; **lodged:** beaten down by wind
58. **warders':** watchmen's
59. **slope:** perhaps, bend, or let fall
62. **nature's germens:** the seeds from which everything springs
63. **sicken:** becomes nauseated (at its own destructiveness)
72. **farrow:** young pigs; **sweaten:** sweated

Winds and "yeasty waves." (4.1.53–55)
From Lodovico Dolce, *Imprese nobili* . . . (1583).

SECOND WITCH
  By the pricking of my thumbs,
  Something wicked this way comes.   45
  Open, locks,
  Whoever knocks.

                    Enter Macbeth.

MACBETH
  How now, you secret, black, and midnight hags?
  What is 't you do?
ALL   A deed without a name.   50
MACBETH
  I conjure you by that which you profess
  (Howe'er you come to know it), answer me.
  Though you untie the winds and let them fight
  Against the churches, though the yeasty waves
  Confound and swallow navigation up,   55
  Though bladed corn be lodged and trees blown
      down,
  Though castles topple on their warders' heads,
  Though palaces and pyramids do slope
  Their heads to their foundations, though the   60
      treasure
  Of nature's ⌜germens⌝ tumble ⌜all together⌝
  Even till destruction sicken, answer me
  To what I ask you.
FIRST WITCH   Speak.   65
SECOND WITCH   Demand.
THIRD WITCH   We'll answer.
FIRST WITCH
  Say if th' hadst rather hear it from our mouths
  Or from our masters'.
MACBETH   Call 'em. Let me see 'em.   70
FIRST WITCH
  Pour in sow's blood that hath eaten
  Her nine farrow; grease that's sweaten

76. **office:** function, duty

76 SD. **Armed Head:** a helmeted **head** (See picture, below.)

84. **harped:** sounded, guessed (as in touching the right string on a harp)

95. **take a bond of fate:** bind **fate** by a contract, get a guarantee from **fate** (i.e., make doubly sure that Macbeth will not be harmed)

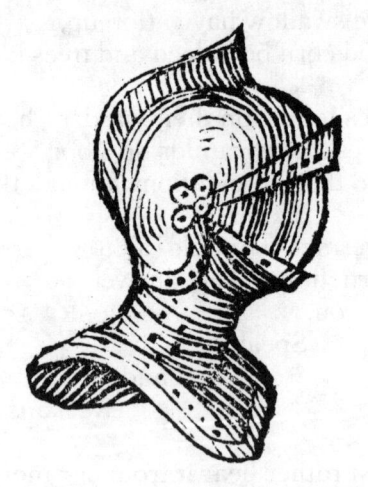

"... an Armed Head." (4.1.76 SD)
From Louis de Gaya, *Traité des armes* ... (1678).

From the murderers' gibbet throw
Into the flame.
ALL   Come high or low;
Thyself and office deftly show.

Thunder. First Apparition, an Armed Head.

MACBETH
Tell me, thou unknown power—
FIRST WITCH   He knows thy
    thought.
Hear his speech but say thou naught.
FIRST APPARITION
Macbeth! Macbeth! Macbeth! Beware Macduff!
Beware the Thane of Fife! Dismiss me. Enough.
                                    He descends.
MACBETH
Whate'er thou art, for thy good caution, thanks.
Thou hast harped my fear aright. But one word
    more—
FIRST WITCH
He will not be commanded. Here's another
More potent than the first.

Thunder. Second Apparition, a Bloody Child.

SECOND APPARITION   Macbeth! Macbeth! Macbeth!—
MACBETH   Had I three ears, I'd hear thee.
SECOND APPARITION
Be bloody, bold, and resolute. Laugh to scorn
The power of man, for none of woman born
Shall harm Macbeth.   ⌜*He*⌝ *descends.*
MACBETH
Then live, Macduff; what need I fear of thee?
But yet I'll make assurance double sure
And take a bond of fate. Thou shalt not live,
That I may tell pale-hearted fear it lies,
And sleep in spite of thunder.

99. **like the issue of a king:** in the shape of an heir to a throne
100–101. **round ... sovereignty:** royal crown
104. **chafes:** becomes irritated
109. **impress:** conscript, draft, compel into service
110. **his:** its; **bodements:** prophecies
111. **Rebellious dead:** perhaps in reference to Banquo, who rebelled against death by appearing to Macbeth
113. **live the lease of nature:** i.e., **live** out his natural life
114. **mortal custom:** normal (customary) death
126. **shadows:** apparitions, illusions (The word could also mean "actors," appropriate for **a show** [line 126 SD].)

A dragon. (4.1.22)
From Ulisse Aldrovandi, ... *Serpentum, et draconum historiae libri duo* ... (1640 [1639]).

Thunder. Third Apparition, a Child Crowned, with a tree in his hand.

                    What is this
    That rises like the issue of a king
    And wears upon his baby brow the round   100
    And top of sovereignty?
ALL   Listen but speak not to 't.
THIRD APPARITION
    Be lion-mettled, proud, and take no care
    Who chafes, who frets, or where conspirers are.
    Macbeth shall never vanquished be until   105
    Great Birnam Wood to high Dunsinane Hill
    Shall come against him.   ⌜*He*⌝ *descends.*
MACBETH   That will never be.
    Who can impress the forest, bid the tree
    Unfix his earthbound root? Sweet bodements, good!   110
    Rebellious dead, rise never till the Wood
    Of Birnam rise, and our high-placed Macbeth
    Shall live the lease of nature, pay his breath
    To time and mortal custom. Yet my heart
    Throbs to know one thing. Tell me, if your art   115
    Can tell so much: shall Banquo's issue ever
    Reign in this kingdom?
ALL   Seek to know no more.
MACBETH
    I will be satisfied. Deny me this,
    And an eternal curse fall on you! Let me know!   120
                 ⌜*Cauldron sinks.*⌝ *Hautboys.*
    Why sinks that cauldron? And what noise is this?
FIRST WITCH   Show.
SECOND WITCH   Show.
THIRD WITCH   Show.
ALL
    Show his eyes and grieve his heart.   125
    Come like shadows; so depart.

126 SD. **show:** (1) spectacle, dumb **show** (stage action without dialogue); (2) manifestation, vision; **eight kings: eight kings** of Scotland, including James VI (a supposed descendant of Banquo), who in 1603 also became James I of England; **glass:** magic mirror or crystal

127–39. **Thou art . . . for his:** Macbeth speaks as the figures walk across the stage one by one, with Banquo appearing last, at line 137.

129. **other:** i.e., second

131. **Start:** i.e., burst from your sockets

132. **th' crack of doom:** perhaps, the thunder crash of judgment day; or, the blast of the archangel's trumpet announcing judgment day

136. **twofold:** double (signifying England and Scotland); **treble:** The reference here is probably to King James's title of "King of Great Britain, France, and Ireland," assumed by him in 1604.

138. **blood-boltered:** i.e., having his hair matted with blood

139. **for his:** as **his** descendants

141–48. **Ay . . . pay:** lines regarded by most scholars as written by another author

142. **amazedly:** as in a trance

143. **sprites:** spirits

146. **antic round:** fantastic dance

150. **aye:** forever

151. **without there:** i.e., you who are outside

A show of eight kings, ⌜the eighth king⌝ with a glass in his hand, and Banquo last.

MACBETH
  Thou art too like the spirit of Banquo. Down!
  Thy crown does sear mine eyeballs. And thy hair,
  Thou other gold-bound brow, is like the first.
  A third is like the former.—Filthy hags, 130
  Why do you show me this?—A fourth? Start, eyes!
  What, will the line stretch out to th' crack of doom?
  Another yet? A seventh? I'll see no more.
  And yet the eighth appears who bears a glass
  Which shows me many more, and some I see 135
  That twofold balls and treble scepters carry.
  Horrible sight! Now I see 'tis true,
  For the blood-boltered Banquo smiles upon me
  And points at them for his.
           ⌜*The Apparitions disappear.*⌝
           What, is this so? 140

FIRST WITCH
  Ay, sir, all this is so. But why
  Stands Macbeth thus amazedly?
  Come, sisters, cheer we up his sprites
  And show the best of our delights.
  I'll charm the air to give a sound 145
  While you perform your antic round,
  That this great king may kindly say
  Our duties did his welcome pay.
           Music. The Witches dance and vanish.

MACBETH
  Where are they? Gone? Let this pernicious hour
  Stand aye accursèd in the calendar!— 150
  Come in, without there.

           Enter Lennox.

LENNOX   What's your Grace's will?

159. **horse:** horses or horsemen

164. **anticipat'st:** prevent, forestall; **dread:** dreadful

165–66. **The flighty purpose...with it:** i.e., purposes are so fleeting that they escape unless accompanied by acts that fulfill them

167. **firstlings:** firstborn

171. **surprise:** seize suddenly

174. **trace him in his line:** i.e., are his descendants

176. **sights:** hallucinations

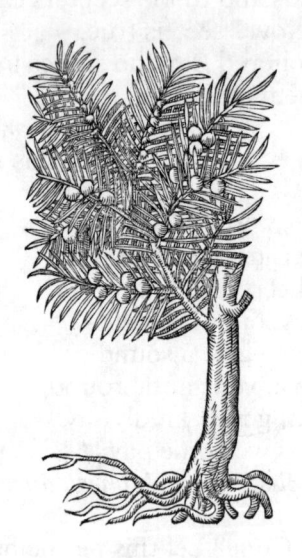

A yew tree. (4.1.27)
From John Gerard, *The herball or generall historie of plantes* ... (1597).

MACBETH
Saw you the Weïrd Sisters?
LENNOX   No, my lord.
MACBETH
Came they not by you?   155
LENNOX   No, indeed, my lord.
MACBETH
Infected be the air whereon they ride,
And damned all those that trust them! I did hear
The galloping of horse. Who was 't came by?
LENNOX
'Tis two or three, my lord, that bring you word   160
Macduff is fled to England.
MACBETH   Fled to England?
LENNOX Ay, my good lord.
MACBETH, ⌜*aside*⌝
Time, thou anticipat'st my dread exploits.
The flighty purpose never is o'ertook   165
Unless the deed go with it. From this moment
The very firstlings of my heart shall be
The firstlings of my hand. And even now,
To crown my thoughts with acts, be it thought and
    done: 170
The castle of Macduff I will surprise,
Seize upon Fife, give to th' edge o' th' sword
His wife, his babes, and all unfortunate souls
That trace him in his line. No boasting like a fool;
This deed I'll do before this purpose cool.   175
But no more sights!—Where are these gentlemen?
Come bring me where they are.
                                            They exit.

4.2 Ross visits Lady Macduff and tries to justify to her Macduff's flight to England, a flight that leaves his family defenseless. After Ross leaves, a messenger arrives to warn Lady Macduff to flee. Before she can do so, Macbeth's men attack her and her son.

---

    5. **Our fears do make us traitors:** perhaps, (Macduff's) fear, leading to his flight, makes him a traitor (to his family? to his country?)
    11. **He wants the natural touch: he** lacks **the natural** instinct (to protect his children)
    13. **Her young ones in her nest:** i.e., when **her young** are **in** the **nest**
    17. **coz:** cousin, kinswoman
    18. **school:** control; **for:** as **for**
    20. **The fits o' th' season:** the violent disturbances in (Scotland's political) climate
    22–23. **we are traitors ... ourselves:** we are considered **traitors** while being unaware of our treason
    23–24. **hold rumor / From what we fear:** perhaps, believe **what** our fears dictate; or judge rumors according to **what we fear** may happen
    27. **Shall not be long but:** i.e., the time will **not be long** before

Scene 2

Enter Macduff's Wife, her Son, and Ross.

LADY MACDUFF
What had he done to make him fly the land?
ROSS
You must have patience, madam.
LADY MACDUFF   He had none.
His flight was madness. When our actions do not,
Our fears do make us traitors.   5
ROSS   You know not
Whether it was his wisdom or his fear.
LADY MACDUFF
Wisdom? To leave his wife, to leave his babes,
His mansion and his titles in a place
From whence himself does fly? He loves us not;   10
He wants the natural touch; for the poor wren,
The most diminutive of birds, will fight,
Her young ones in her nest, against the owl.
All is the fear, and nothing is the love,
As little is the wisdom, where the flight   15
So runs against all reason.
ROSS   My dearest coz,
I pray you school yourself. But for your husband,
He is noble, wise, judicious, and best knows
The fits o' th' season. I dare not speak much   20
   further;
But cruel are the times when we are traitors
And do not know ourselves; when we hold rumor
From what we fear, yet know not what we fear,
But float upon a wild and violent sea   25
Each way and move—I take my leave of you.
Shall not be long but I'll be here again.
Things at the worst will cease or else climb upward
To what they were before.—My pretty cousin,
Blessing upon you.   30

32–33. **should . . . discomfort:** i.e., if **I should stay longer,** (my tears) **would** disgrace me and make you uncomfortable

37. **As birds do:** See Matthew 6.26: "Behold the fowls of the air; for they sow not, neither do they reap . . . ; yet your heavenly Father feedeth them."

40–41. **the net nor lime, / The pitfall nor the gin:** traps for catching birds   **lime:** birdlime   **gin:** snare (literally, "engine") (See picture, below.)

42–43. **Poor birds . . . set for:** i.e., people don't **set** traps **for** *poor* **birds** (**birds** of little worth)—wordplay on Lady Macduff's **Poor bird** (**bird** that is pitiable or unfortunate), line 40

49. **wit:** intelligence

50. **for thee:** for a child

54. **swears and lies:** Lady Macduff defines a traitor as **one** who **swears** an oath of loyalty to a sovereign and then breaks it; the oath, then, is a lie. Her son seems to take "swearing and lying" as general use of profanity and failing to tell the truth.

Birds caught in a "gin" or trap. (4.2.40–41)
From Henry Parrot, *Laquei ridiculosi* . . . (1613).

LADY MACDUFF
Fathered he is, and yet he's fatherless.
ROSS
I am so much a fool, should I stay longer
It would be my disgrace and your discomfort.
I take my leave at once. *Ross exits.*
LADY MACDUFF Sirrah, your father's dead.
And what will you do now? How will you live?
SON
As birds do, mother.
LADY MACDUFF   What, with worms and flies?
SON
With what I get, I mean; and so do they.
LADY MACDUFF
Poor bird, thou'dst never fear the net nor lime,
The pitfall nor the gin.
SON
Why should I, mother? Poor birds they are not set
  for.
My father is not dead, for all your saying.
LADY MACDUFF
Yes, he is dead. How wilt thou do for a father?
SON Nay, how will you do for a husband?
LADY MACDUFF
Why, I can buy me twenty at any market.
SON Then you'll buy 'em to sell again.
LADY MACDUFF Thou speak'st with all thy wit,
And yet, i' faith, with wit enough for thee.
SON Was my father a traitor, mother?
LADY MACDUFF Ay, that he was.
SON What is a traitor?
LADY MACDUFF Why, one that swears and lies.
SON And be all traitors that do so?
LADY MACDUFF Every one that does so is a traitor and
  must be hanged.
SON And must they all be hanged that swear and lie?

72. **in your state of honor I am perfect:** I know you well as a noble lady
73. **doubt:** fear; **nearly:** very soon; very near
74. **homely:** plain
77. **do worse:** i.e., physically abuse you; **fell:** terrible
78. **Which is too nigh:** i.e., such savage cruelty is all too near

An earthquake. (2.3.68–69)
From Conrad Lycosthenes, *Prodigiorum* (1557).

LADY MACDUFF Every one.
SON Who must hang them? 60
LADY MACDUFF Why, the honest men.
SON Then the liars and swearers are fools, for there are liars and swearers enough to beat the honest men and hang up them.
LADY MACDUFF Now God help thee, poor monkey! But 65
how wilt thou do for a father?
SON If he were dead, you'd weep for him. If you would not, it were a good sign that I should quickly have a new father.
LADY MACDUFF Poor prattler, how thou talk'st! 70

Enter a Messenger.

MESSENGER
Bless you, fair dame. I am not to you known,
Though in your state of honor I am perfect.
I doubt some danger does approach you nearly.
If you will take a homely man's advice,
Be not found here. Hence with your little ones! 75
To fright you thus methinks I am too savage;
To do worse to you were fell cruelty,
Which is too nigh your person. Heaven preserve
  you!
I dare abide no longer. *Messenger exits.* 80
LADY MACDUFF Whither should I fly?
I have done no harm. But I remember now
I am in this earthly world, where to do harm
Is often laudable, to do good sometime
Accounted dangerous folly. Why then, alas, 85
Do I put up that womanly defense
To say I have done no harm?

Enter Murderers.

                    What are these faces?
MURDERER Where is your husband?

93. **shag-eared:** changed by many editors to "shag-haired"
   94. **egg:** term of contempt for a child
   95. **fry:** offspring, progeny

4.3 Macduff finds Malcolm at the English court and urges him to attack Macbeth at once. Malcolm suspects that Macduff is Macbeth's agent sent to lure Malcolm to his destruction in Scotland. After Malcolm tests Macduff and finds him sincere, Malcolm reveals that Edward, king of England, has provided a commander (Siward) and ten thousand troops for the invasion of Scotland. Ross then arrives with the news of the slaughter of Macduff's entire household. At first grief-stricken, Macduff follows Malcolm's advice and converts his grief into a desire to avenge himself on Macbeth.

───────────

   4. **mortal:** deadly; **good men:** i.e., strong fighting men
   5. **Bestride ... birthdom:** i.e., fight to protect our prostrated country (The image is that of a soldier straddling a felled comrade and fighting off the comrade's attackers.)
   7. **that:** i.e., so **that**
   9. **Like syllable:** the same (or a comparable) sound
   12. **the time to friend:** an opportune (friendly) time
   14. **sole:** mere
   15. **honest:** honorable

LADY MACDUFF
  I hope in no place so unsanctified   90
  Where such as thou mayst find him.
MURDERER   He's a traitor.
SON
  Thou liest, thou shag-eared villain!
MURDERER   What, you egg?
  ⌜Stabbing him.⌝ Young fry of treachery!   95
SON   He has killed
    me, mother.
  Run away, I pray you.
  ⌜Lady Macduff⌝ exits, crying "Murder!" ⌜followed by the
                        Murderers bearing the Son's body.⌝

                        Scene 3

              Enter Malcolm and Macduff.

MALCOLM
  Let us seek out some desolate shade and there
  Weep our sad bosoms empty.
MACDUFF   Let us rather
  Hold fast the mortal sword and, like good men,
  Bestride our ⌜downfall'n⌝ birthdom. Each new morn   5
  New widows howl, new orphans cry, new sorrows
  Strike heaven on the face, that it resounds
  As if it felt with Scotland, and yelled out
  Like syllable of dolor.
MALCOLM   What I believe, I'll wail;   10
  What know, believe; and what I can redress,
  As I shall find the time to friend, I will.
  What you have spoke, it may be so, perchance.
  This tyrant, whose sole name blisters our tongues,
  Was once thought honest. You have loved him well.   15
  He hath not touched you yet. I am young, but
    something

18. **and wisdom:** i.e., **and** consider it **wisdom**

23–24. **recoil / In an imperial charge:** The general sense is "give way under pressure from a king." **recoil:** fall back, degenerate **charge:** mandate, order

26. **That ... transpose:** i.e., **my thoughts** (no matter how negative) **cannot** change you into something different from what **you are**

27. **the brightest:** i.e., Lucifer, brightest of the angels, cast from heaven for rebelling against God

28–30. **Though ... so:** i.e., even though **foul things** wear, when they can, the look of those in a state **of grace,** those really in a state **of grace** nevertheless continue to **look** gracious

32. **even there:** in the very place

33. **rawness:** vulnerability, unprotectedness

34. **motives:** (1) incitements (to his protective instinct); (2) arguments (for his protection)

36–37. **Let ... safeties:** i.e., don't assume that my suspicions cast doubts on your honor, but see them as measures taken for my own safety **jealousies:** suspicions

37. **rightly just:** perfectly honorable

40. **basis:** foundation; **sure:** securely, safely

41. **check:** restrain, reprove, curb

41–42. **Wear thou thy wrongs:** i.e., carry (as an heraldic device on your shield) that which you have won through your crimes

43. **The title is affeered:** i.e., Macbeth's **title** to the crown **is** confirmed (**affeered**)

48. **absolute fear:** complete mistrust

51. **withal:** as well, at the same time

140

You may ⌜deserve⌝ of him through me, and wisdom
To offer up a weak, poor, innocent lamb
T' appease an angry god.   20
MACDUFF
I am not treacherous.
MALCOLM   But Macbeth is.
A good and virtuous nature may recoil
In an imperial charge. But I shall crave your
    pardon.   25
That which you are, my thoughts cannot transpose.
Angels are bright still, though the brightest fell.
Though all things foul would wear the brows of
    grace,
Yet grace must still look so.   30
MACDUFF   I have lost my hopes.
MALCOLM
Perchance even there where I did find my doubts.
Why in that rawness left you wife and child,
Those precious motives, those strong knots of love,
Without leave-taking? I pray you,   35
Let not my jealousies be your dishonors,
But mine own safeties. You may be rightly just,
Whatever I shall think.
MACDUFF   Bleed, bleed, poor country!
Great tyranny, lay thou thy basis sure,   40
For goodness dare not check thee. Wear thou thy
    wrongs;
The title is affeered.—Fare thee well, lord.
I would not be the villain that thou think'st
For the whole space that's in the tyrant's grasp, 45
And the rich East to boot.
MALCOLM   Be not offended.
I speak not as in absolute fear of you.
I think our country sinks beneath the yoke.
It weeps, it bleeds, and each new day a gash   50
Is added to her wounds. I think withal

53. **gracious England:** the **gracious** king of England
58. **More suffer:** shall **suffer more**
59. **succeed:** i.e., **succeed** to the throne
62. **particulars:** various kinds; **grafted:** implanted, engrafted
63. **opened:** exposed; or, unfolded like a flower
66. **confineless:** unbounded
69. **top:** surpass
70. **bloody:** bloodthirsty
71. **Luxurious:** lecherous
72. **Sudden:** rash
75. **maids:** virgins
77. **continent:** chaste; also, restraining
78. **will:** lust, carnal appetite
83. **yet:** nevertheless
85. **Convey ... plenty:** secretly conduct **your pleasures** on a large scale **Convey:** manage **spacious:** ample
86. **cold:** chaste; or, indifferent; **hoodwink:** delude, blindfold

There would be hands uplifted in my right;
And here from gracious England have I offer
Of goodly thousands. But, for all this,
When I shall tread upon the tyrant's head 55
Or wear it on my sword, yet my poor country
Shall have more vices than it had before,
More suffer, and more sundry ways than ever,
By him that shall succeed.
MACDUFF What should he be? 60
MALCOLM
It is myself I mean, in whom I know
All the particulars of vice so grafted
That, when they shall be opened, black Macbeth
Will seem as pure as snow, and the poor state
Esteem him as a lamb, being compared 65
With my confineless harms.
MACDUFF Not in the legions
Of horrid hell can come a devil more damned
In evils to top Macbeth.
MALCOLM I grant him bloody, 70
Luxurious, avaricious, false, deceitful,
Sudden, malicious, smacking of every sin
That has a name. But there's no bottom, none,
In my voluptuousness. Your wives, your daughters,
Your matrons, and your maids could not fill up 75
The cistern of my lust, and my desire
All continent impediments would o'erbear
That did oppose my will. Better Macbeth
Than such an one to reign.
MACDUFF Boundless intemperance 80
In nature is a tyranny. It hath been
Th' untimely emptying of the happy throne
And fall of many kings. But fear not yet
To take upon you what is yours. You may
Convey your pleasures in a spacious plenty 85
And yet seem cold—the time you may so hoodwink.

92. **affection:** disposition
93. **stanchless:** insatiable
94. **cut off:** destroy, kill
95. **his jewels:** the **jewels** of one subject
102. **summer-seeming:** i.e., summer-beseeming, suitable for the summer of one's youth; or, summer-like and therefore of short duration
103. **The sword . . . kings:** i.e., the cause of the death **of our slain kings**
104. **foisons:** plentiful supplies
105. **Of your mere own:** from your royal property alone; **portable:** bearable, supportable
106. **With . . . weighed:** balanced against **other** qualities that are virtuous
108. **As:** such **as**
109. **lowliness:** humility
111. **relish of:** taste for; trace of
112. **division:** variation, modulation (as if each crime were a piece of music to be played); **several:** distinct
115. **confound:** destroy

We have willing dames enough. There cannot be
That vulture in you to devour so many
As will to greatness dedicate themselves,
Finding it so inclined.

MALCOLM   With this there grows
In my most ill-composed affection such
A stanchless avarice that, were I king,
I should cut off the nobles for their lands,
Desire his jewels, and this other's house;
And my more-having would be as a sauce
To make me hunger more, that I should forge
Quarrels unjust against the good and loyal,
Destroying them for wealth.

MACDUFF   This avarice
Sticks deeper, grows with more pernicious root
Than summer-seeming lust, and it hath been
The sword of our slain kings. Yet do not fear.
Scotland hath foisons to fill up your will
Of your mere own. All these are portable,
With other graces weighed.

MALCOLM
But I have none. The king-becoming graces,
As justice, verity, temp'rance, stableness,
Bounty, perseverance, mercy, lowliness,
Devotion, patience, courage, fortitude,
I have no relish of them but abound
In the division of each several crime,
Acting it many ways. Nay, had I power, I should
Pour the sweet milk of concord into hell,
Uproar the universal peace, confound
All unity on earth.

MACDUFF   O Scotland, Scotland!

MALCOLM
If such a one be fit to govern, speak.
I am as I have spoken.

MACDUFF   Fit to govern?

122. **untitled:** i.e., unentitled, usurping
124. **truest issue of thy throne:** heir with the most right to the **throne**
125. **interdiction:** i.e., censure
126. **blaspheme his breed:** defame his family line (through his scandalous behavior)
129. **Died... lived:** died to the world (mortified her flesh through penances and religious exercises) **every day** of her life
133. **passion:** display of feelings
137. **trains:** wiles, stratagems (such as Macduff's visit seemed to be); **win:** capture, seize
138. **modest wisdom:** wise moderation, prudent caution; **plucks me:** pulls me back
142. **mine own detraction: my detraction** of myself
144. **For:** as
145. **Unknown to woman:** i.e., a virgin (rather than the lascivious beast that I presented myself as being); **never was forsworn:** have **never** deliberately broken my oath
150. **upon:** about
153. **warlike:** equipped for battle
154. **at a point:** in readiness
155–56. **we'll... quarrel:** i.e., we will travel **together,** and may our success be as good as our cause is just   **chance of goodness:** success   **warranted:** justified   **quarrel:** ground for action

No, not to live.—O nation miserable,
With an untitled tyrant bloody-sceptered,
When shalt thou see thy wholesome days again,
Since that the truest issue of thy throne
By his own interdiction stands ⌜accursed⌝ 125
And does blaspheme his breed?—Thy royal father
Was a most sainted king. The queen that bore thee,
Oft'ner upon her knees than on her feet,
Died every day she lived. Fare thee well.
These evils thou repeat'st upon thyself 130
Hath banished me from Scotland.—O my breast,
Thy hope ends here!

MALCOLM   Macduff, this noble passion,
Child of integrity, hath from my soul
Wiped the black scruples, reconciled my thoughts 135
To thy good truth and honor. Devilish Macbeth
By many of these trains hath sought to win me
Into his power, and modest wisdom plucks me
From overcredulous haste. But God above
Deal between thee and me, for even now 140
I put myself to thy direction and
Unspeak mine own detraction, here abjure
The taints and blames I laid upon myself
For strangers to my nature. I am yet
Unknown to woman, never was forsworn, 145
Scarcely have coveted what was mine own,
At no time broke my faith, would not betray
The devil to his fellow, and delight
No less in truth than life. My first false speaking
Was this upon myself. What I am truly 150
Is thine and my poor country's to command—
Whither indeed, before ⌜thy here-approach,⌝
Old Siward with ten thousand warlike men,
Already at a point, was setting forth.
Now we'll together, and the chance of goodness 155
Be like our warranted quarrel. Why are you silent?

159. **forth:** i.e., out of his private rooms
162. **stay:** await
162–63. **convinces ... art:** conquers (defeats) the efforts of (medical) science
165. **presently:** immediately
168. **the evil:** i.e., scrofula, or "**the** king's **evil,**" so-called because the king was thought to have the power to heal it with his touch
172. **strangely visited:** i.e., afflicted by this strange disease
174. **mere:** total, utter
175. **stamp:** a coin stamped with a particular impression
177–78. **To the succeeding royalty ... benediction:** i.e., **to the** royal line that will succeed him **he** bequeaths the power of giving this curative blessing
178. **With:** along **with; virtue:** power
183. **My ... not:** i.e., I can tell (by his clothing) that he is from Scotland, **but** I do not **yet** recognize him

MACDUFF
  Such welcome and unwelcome things at once
  'Tis hard to reconcile.

            Enter a Doctor.

MALCOLM   Well, more anon.—
  Comes the King forth, I pray you?
DOCTOR
  Ay, sir. There are a crew of wretched souls
  That stay his cure. Their malady convinces
  The great assay of art, but at his touch
  (Such sanctity hath heaven given his hand)
  They presently amend.
MALCOLM   I thank you, doctor.
                    ⌜*Doctor*⌝ *exits.*

MACDUFF
  What's the disease he means?
MALCOLM   'Tis called the evil:
  A most miraculous work in this good king,
  Which often since my here-remain in England
  I have seen him do. How he solicits heaven
  Himself best knows, but strangely visited people
  All swoll'n and ulcerous, pitiful to the eye,
  The mere despair of surgery, he cures,
  Hanging a golden stamp about their necks,
  Put on with holy prayers; and, 'tis spoken,
  To the succeeding royalty he leaves
  The healing benediction. With this strange virtue,
  He hath a heavenly gift of prophecy,
  And sundry blessings hang about his throne
  That speak him full of grace.

            Enter Ross.

MACDUFF   See who comes here.
MALCOLM
  My countryman, but yet I know him ⌜not.⌝

185. **betimes:** soon
192. **But who:** except someone who; **once:** ever
193. **rent:** rend, tear
194. **made, not marked:** i.e., so common as not to be noted
195. **modern:** ordinary, commonplace; **ecstasy:** i.e., emotion
198. **or ere they:** before they ever
199. **relation:** report; **nice:** precisely spelled out
200. **grief:** wrong, injury
201. **doth hiss the speaker:** i.e., earns the teller of the injury only hisses because it is already an old story
202. **teems:** brings forth
204. **well:** When spoken of the dead, **well** meant "at peace." The proverb ran: "He is **well** since he is in Heaven." See *Antony and Cleopatra* 2.5.38–39: "we use / To say the dead are **well**"; *Romeo and Juliet* 5.1.18–19: "she is **well** . . . / Her body sleeps in Capels' monument."
209. **niggard:** miser

150

MACDUFF
  My ever-gentle cousin, welcome hither.
MALCOLM
  I know him now.—Good God betimes remove   185
  The means that makes us strangers!
ROSS   Sir, amen.
MACDUFF
  Stands Scotland where it did?
ROSS   Alas, poor country,
  Almost afraid to know itself. It cannot   190
  Be called our mother, but our grave, where nothing
  But who knows nothing is once seen to smile;
  Where sighs and groans and shrieks that rent the air
  Are made, not marked; where violent sorrow seems
  A modern ecstasy. The dead man's knell   195
  Is there scarce asked for who, and good men's lives
  Expire before the flowers in their caps,
  Dying or ere they sicken.
MACDUFF
  O relation too nice and yet too true!
MALCOLM   What's the newest grief?   200
ROSS
  That of an hour's age doth hiss the speaker.
  Each minute teems a new one.
MACDUFF   How does my wife?
ROSS   Why, well.
MACDUFF   And all my children?   205
ROSS   Well too.
MACDUFF
  The tyrant has not battered at their peace?
ROSS
  No, they were well at peace when I did leave 'em.
MACDUFF
  Be not a niggard of your speech. How goes 't?
ROSS
  When I came hither to transport the tidings   210

212. **out:** i.e., in arms, in rebellion
213–14. **witnessed the rather / For that:** confirmed the more readily because
214. **power:** forces; **afoot:** mobilized
215. **of:** for; **Your eye:** i.e., Malcolm's person
217. **doff:** put off, get rid of
221–22. **An older . . . gives out:** i.e., there is no one in the Christian world reputed to be a more experienced or **better soldier   none:** there is **none   gives out:** proclaims
225. **would:** ought to
226. **latch:** catch the sound of
229–30. **a fee-grief / Due to some single breast:** a grief belonging to one particular person   **fee-grief:** a term modeled on the term "fee-simple," an estate belonging to one man and his heirs forever   **Due to:** belonging to
240. **surprised:** captured without warning
242. **quarry:** heap

Which I have heavily borne, there ran a rumor
Of many worthy fellows that were out;
Which was to my belief witnessed the rather
For that I saw the tyrant's power afoot.
Now is the time of help. Your eye in Scotland   215
Would create soldiers, make our women fight
To doff their dire distresses.
MALCOLM   Be 't their comfort
We are coming thither. Gracious England hath
Lent us good Siward and ten thousand men;   220
An older and a better soldier none
That Christendom gives out.
ROSS   Would I could answer
This comfort with the like. But I have words
That would be howled out in the desert air,   225
Where hearing should not latch them.
MACDUFF   What concern
  they—
The general cause, or is it a fee-grief
Due to some single breast?   230
ROSS   No mind that's honest
But in it shares some woe, though the main part
Pertains to you alone.
MACDUFF   If it be mine,
Keep it not from me. Quickly let me have it.   235
ROSS
Let not your ears despise my tongue forever,
Which shall possess them with the heaviest sound
That ever yet they heard.
MACDUFF   Hum! I guess at it.
ROSS
Your castle is surprised, your wife and babes   240
Savagely slaughtered. To relate the manner
Were on the quarry of these murdered deer
To add the death of you.
MALCOLM   Merciful heaven!

245. **pull... brows:** a conventional gesture of deep sorrow

246–47. **The grief... break:** Proverbial: "**Grief** pent up will **break the heart.**" **Whispers: whispers** to **o'erfraught:** overburdened

250. **from thence:** away from there

255. **He has no children:** Usually taken to mean that Macbeth's lack of children explains his unspeakable cruelty, the words could mean that *Malcolm*'s lack of children explains his rather callous attempts to cheer up Macduff.

256. **hell-kite:** evil bird of prey

259. **Dispute:** fight against

265. **Naught that I am:** i.e., wicked man **that I am**

270. **play the woman with mine eyes:** i.e., weep

272. **intermission:** delay; **Front to front:** i.e., face to face

What, man, ne'er pull your hat upon your brows. 245
Give sorrow words. The grief that does not speak
Whispers the o'erfraught heart and bids it break.
MACDUFF   My children too?
ROSS
   Wife, children, servants, all that could be found.
MACDUFF
   And I must be from thence? My wife killed too?   250
   ROSS   I have said.
   MALCOLM   Be comforted.
   Let's make us med'cines of our great revenge
   To cure this deadly grief.
MACDUFF
   He has no children. All my pretty ones?   255
   Did you say "all"? O hell-kite! All?
   What, all my pretty chickens and their dam
   At one fell swoop?
   MALCOLM   Dispute it like a man.
   MACDUFF   I shall do so,   260
   But I must also feel it as a man.
   I cannot but remember such things were
   That were most precious to me. Did heaven look on
   And would not take their part? Sinful Macduff,
   They were all struck for thee! Naught that I am,   265
   Not for their own demerits, but for mine,
   Fell slaughter on their souls. Heaven rest them now.
MALCOLM
   Be this the whetstone of your sword. Let grief
   Convert to anger. Blunt not the heart; enrage it.
MACDUFF
   O, I could play the woman with mine eyes   270
   And braggart with my tongue! But, gentle heavens,
   Cut short all intermission! Front to front
   Bring thou this fiend of Scotland and myself.
   Within my sword's length set him. If he 'scape,
   Heaven forgive him too.   275

278. **Our ... leave:** we lack **nothing** now except to take **leave** (of the king)
279. **powers:** (1) gods; (2) troops, armies, hosts
280. **Put on their instruments:** i.e., arm themselves for battle **instruments:** weapons

A knight in armor. (5.3.43–44, 59; 5.5.59)
From Henry Peacham, *Minerua Britanna* (1612).

MALCOLM   This ⌜tune⌝ goes manly.
Come, go we to the King. Our power is ready;
Our lack is nothing but our leave. Macbeth
Is ripe for shaking, and the powers above
Put on their instruments. Receive what cheer you
  may.
The night is long that never finds the day.
They exit.

The Tragedy of
MACBETH

ACT 5

5.1 A gentlewoman who waits on Lady Macbeth has seen her walking in her sleep and has asked a doctor's advice. Together they observe Lady Macbeth make the gestures of repeatedly washing her hands as she relives the horrors that she and Macbeth have carried out and experienced. The doctor concludes that she needs spiritual rather than medical aid.

---

  0 SD. **Physic:** medicine
  3. **walked:** i.e., **walked** in her sleep
  5–6. **nightgown:** dressing gown
  6. **closet:** cabinet
  11–12. **do the effects of watching:** perform the actions of (someone) awake
  17. **meet:** proper
  21. **very guise:** usual behavior
  22. **close:** hidden

ACT 5

Scene 1

Enter a Doctor of Physic and a Waiting-Gentlewoman.

DOCTOR I have two nights watched with you but can perceive no truth in your report. When was it she last walked?

GENTLEWOMAN Since his Majesty went into the field, I have seen her rise from her bed, throw her nightgown upon her, unlock her closet, take forth paper, fold it, write upon 't, read it, afterwards seal it, and again return to bed; yet all this while in a most fast sleep.

DOCTOR A great perturbation in nature, to receive at once the benefit of sleep and do the effects of watching. In this slumb'ry agitation, besides her walking and other actual performances, what at any time have you heard her say?

GENTLEWOMAN That, sir, which I will not report after her.

DOCTOR You may to me, and 'tis most meet you should.

GENTLEWOMAN Neither to you nor anyone, having no witness to confirm my speech.

Enter Lady ⌜Macbeth⌝ with a taper.

Lo you, here she comes. This is her very guise and, upon my life, fast asleep. Observe her; stand close.

30. **accustomed:** customary, usual
37. **One. Two.:** She is presumably remembering the clock striking 2 A.M. just before the murder.
43. **mark:** hear, notice
46. **mar all:** upset everything
47. **this starting:** these starts (i.e., sudden fits)
48. **Go to:** for shame
56–57. **sorely charged:** gravely burdened
59. **dignity:** worth

DOCTOR How came she by that light?
GENTLEWOMAN Why, it stood by her. She has light by
    her continually. 'Tis her command.   25
DOCTOR You see her eyes are open.
GENTLEWOMAN Ay, but their sense are shut.
DOCTOR What is it she does now? Look how she rubs
    her hands.
GENTLEWOMAN It is an accustomed action with her to   30
    seem thus washing her hands. I have known her
    continue in this a quarter of an hour.
LADY MACBETH Yet here's a spot.
DOCTOR Hark, she speaks. I will set down what comes
    from her, to satisfy my remembrance the more   35
    strongly.
LADY MACBETH Out, damned spot, out, I say! One. Two.
    Why then, 'tis time to do 't. Hell is murky. Fie, my
    lord, fie, a soldier and afeard? What need we fear
    who knows it, when none can call our power to   40
    account? Yet who would have thought the old man
    to have had so much blood in him?
DOCTOR Do you mark that?
LADY MACBETH The Thane of Fife had a wife. Where is
    she now? What, will these hands ne'er be clean? No   45
    more o' that, my lord, no more o' that. You mar all
    with this starting.
DOCTOR Go to, go to. You have known what you should
    not.
GENTLEWOMAN She has spoke what she should not,   50
    I am sure of that. Heaven knows what she has
    known.
LADY MACBETH Here's the smell of the blood still. All
    the perfumes of Arabia will not sweeten this little
    hand. O, O, O!   55
DOCTOR What a sigh is there! The heart is sorely
    charged.
GENTLEWOMAN I would not have such a heart in my
    bosom for the dignity of the whole body.

65–66. **nightgown:** dressing gown
67. **on 's:** of his
78. **divine:** minister or priest
80. **annoyance:** i.e., injuring herself
82. **mated:** stupefied; **amazed:** astounded

5.2 A Scottish force, in rebellion against Macbeth, marches toward Birnam Wood to join Malcolm and his English army.

---

0 SD. **Drum and Colors:** i.e., a drummer and men carrying banners

A Scottish castle with moat, drawbridge, and towers. (5.2.14)
From Raphael Holinshed, *The historie of Scotland* (1577).

DOCTOR Well, well, well.
GENTLEWOMAN Pray God it be, sir.
DOCTOR This disease is beyond my practice. Yet I have known those which have walked in their sleep, who have died holily in their beds.
LADY MACBETH Wash your hands. Put on your nightgown. Look not so pale. I tell you yet again, Banquo's buried; he cannot come out on 's grave.
DOCTOR Even so?
LADY MACBETH To bed, to bed. There's knocking at the gate. Come, come, come, come. Give me your hand. What's done cannot be undone. To bed, to bed, to bed. *Lady ⌜Macbeth⌝ exits.*
DOCTOR Will she go now to bed?
GENTLEWOMAN Directly.
DOCTOR
  Foul whisp'rings are abroad. Unnatural deeds
  Do breed unnatural troubles. Infected minds
  To their deaf pillows will discharge their secrets.
  More needs she the divine than the physician.
  God, God forgive us all. Look after her.
  Remove from her the means of all annoyance
  And still keep eyes upon her. So, good night.
  My mind she has mated, and amazed my sight.
  I think but dare not speak.
GENTLEWOMAN   Good night, good doctor.
               They exit.

Scene 2

Drum and Colors. Enter Menteith, Caithness, Angus, Lennox, ⌜and⌝ Soldiers.

MENTEITH
  The English power is near, led on by Malcolm,
  His uncle Siward, and the good Macduff.

3. **dear:** deeply felt; also, grievous, dire
4–5. **Would . . . man:** i.e., **would** quicken dead men to bloody and desperate attack   **alarm:** call to fight   **Excite:** quicken   **mortified:** dead
9. **file:** list
11. **unrough:** unbearded, smooth-faced
12. **Protest:** assert; **their first of manhood:** the beginning of **their manhood**
17. **distempered:** diseased and swollen
21. **minutely:** i.e., every minute; **upbraid:** condemn; **faith-breach:** breach of his oath (to Duncan—or breach of all oaths and vows)
27. **pestered:** infested; obstructed; overcrowded; **to recoil and start:** to flinch in alarm
32. **weal:** state, commonwealth
33–34. **pour . . . us:** i.e., **pour** out every drop of our blood in purging (curing) our country

Revenges burn in them, for their dear causes
Would to the bleeding and the grim alarm
Excite the mortified man.   5
ANGUS   Near Birnam Wood
    Shall we well meet them. That way are they coming.
CAITHNESS
    Who knows if Donalbain be with his brother?
LENNOX
    For certain, sir, he is not. I have a file
    Of all the gentry. There is Siward's son   10
    And many unrough youths that even now
    Protest their first of manhood.
MENTEITH   What does the tyrant?
CAITHNESS
    Great Dunsinane he strongly fortifies.
    Some say he's mad; others that lesser hate him   15
    Do call it valiant fury. But for certain
    He cannot buckle his distempered cause
    Within the belt of rule.
ANGUS   Now does he feel
    His secret murders sticking on his hands.   20
    Now minutely revolts upbraid his faith-breach.
    Those he commands move only in command,
    Nothing in love. Now does he feel his title
    Hang loose about him, like a giant's robe
    Upon a dwarfish thief.   25
MENTEITH   Who, then, shall blame
    His pestered senses to recoil and start
    When all that is within him does condemn
    Itself for being there?
CAITHNESS   Well, march we on   30
    To give obedience where 'tis truly owed.
    Meet we the med'cine of the sickly weal,
    And with him pour we in our country's purge
    Each drop of us.
LENNOX   Or so much as it needs   35

5.3 Reports are brought to Macbeth of the Scottish and English forces massed against him. He seeks assurance in the apparitions' promise of safety for himself. But he is anxious about Lady Macbeth's condition and impatient with her doctor's inability to cure her.

---

 1. **them fly all:** i.e., the deserting thanes **all** flee
 3. **taint:** become tainted
 5. **mortal consequences:** that which happens to humanity
 9. **English epicures:** a Scottish taunt at **English** eating habits   **epicures:** gluttons, or those devoted to luxury
 10. **sway by:** rule myself by
 12. **loon:** rogue
 17. **over-red thy fear:** i.e., give color to your frightened face
 18. **lily-livered:** white-livered (because bloodless), cowardly; **patch:** fool
 19. **of thy:** on your
 20. **Are counselors to fear:** i.e., teach others to be frightened
 24. **push:** effort

To dew the sovereign flower and drown the weeds.
Make we our march towards Birnam.
They exit marching.

Scene 3

Enter Macbeth, ⌜the⌝ Doctor, and Attendants.

MACBETH
Bring me no more reports. Let them fly all.
Till Birnam Wood remove to Dunsinane
I cannot taint with fear. What's the boy Malcolm?
Was he not born of woman? The spirits that know
All mortal consequences have pronounced me thus: 5
"Fear not, Macbeth. No man that's born of woman
Shall e'er have power upon thee." Then fly, false
thanes,
And mingle with the English epicures.
The mind I sway by and the heart I bear 10
Shall never sag with doubt nor shake with fear.

Enter Servant.

The devil damn thee black, thou cream-faced loon!
Where got'st thou that goose-look?
SERVANT There is ten thousand—
MACBETH Geese, villain? 15
SERVANT Soldiers, sir.
MACBETH
Go prick thy face and over-red thy fear,
Thou lily-livered boy. What soldiers, patch?
Death of thy soul! Those linen cheeks of thine
Are counselors to fear. What soldiers, whey-face? 20
SERVANT The English force, so please you.
MACBETH
Take thy face hence. ⌜*Servant exits.*⌝
Seyton!—I am sick at heart
When I behold—Seyton, I say!—This push

25. **disseat:** unseat, dethrone
  27. **the sere:** the (condition of being) dry and withered
  29. **As:** such as
  30. **look:** expect
  31. **mouth-honor:** honor from the tongue (rather than the heart); **breath:** voice (of support)
  32. **fain:** gladly
  42. **Skirr:** search quickly, scour
  52. **Raze out:** erase
  53. **oblivious:** i.e., causing oblivion
  54. **stuffed:** clogged

A warrior's armor. (5.3.39,43–44)
From Wilhelm Dilich, . . . *Krieges-Schule* . . . (1689).

Will cheer me ever or ⌜disseat⌝ me now.
I have lived long enough. My way of life
Is fall'n into the sere, the yellow leaf,
And that which should accompany old age,
As honor, love, obedience, troops of friends,
I must not look to have, but in their stead
Curses, not loud but deep, mouth-honor, breath
Which the poor heart would fain deny and dare
    not.—
Seyton!

Enter Seyton.

SEYTON
What's your gracious pleasure?
MACBETH   What news more?
SEYTON
All is confirmed, my lord, which was reported.
MACBETH
I'll fight till from my bones my flesh be hacked.
Give me my armor.
SEYTON 'Tis not needed yet.
MACBETH I'll put it on.
Send out more horses. Skirr the country round.
Hang those that talk of fear. Give me mine
    armor.—
How does your patient, doctor?
DOCTOR Not so sick, my lord,
As she is troubled with thick-coming fancies
That keep her from her rest.
MACBETH   Cure ⌜her⌝ of that.
Canst thou not minister to a mind diseased,
Pluck from the memory a rooted sorrow,
Raze out the written troubles of the brain,
And with some sweet oblivious antidote
Cleanse the stuffed bosom of that perilous stuff
Which weighs upon the heart?

58. **physic:** medicine
62. **dispatch:** make haste (probably said to one of his attendants who is arming him)
62–63. **cast / The water of my land:** i.e., diagnose the disease from which Scotland is suffering **cast the water:** examine the (patient's) urine to diagnose an illness
69. **them:** i.e., the English
73. **bane:** destruction

5.4 The rebel Scottish forces have joined Malcolm's army at Birnam Wood. Malcolm orders each soldier to cut down and carry a bough from the Wood so as to conceal their numbers from Macbeth.

1. **Cousins:** kinsmen
2. **chambers:** i.e., such rooms as bedchambers and dining rooms (See 1.7.31, where the dining hall of Inverness is called a **chamber.**)

DOCTOR
                              Therein the patient
  Must minister to himself.
MACBETH
  Throw physic to the dogs. I'll none of it.—
  Come, put mine armor on. Give me my staff.
                    ⌜*Attendants begin to arm him.*⌝
  Seyton, send out.—Doctor, the thanes fly from   60
    me.—
  Come, sir, dispatch.—If thou couldst, doctor, cast
  The water of my land, find her disease,
  And purge it to a sound and pristine health,
  I would applaud thee to the very echo   65
  That should applaud again.—Pull 't off, I say.—
  What rhubarb, senna, or what purgative drug
  Would scour these English hence? Hear'st thou of
    them?
DOCTOR
  Ay, my good lord. Your royal preparation   70
  Makes us hear something.
MACBETH   Bring it after me.—
  I will not be afraid of death and bane
  Till Birnam Forest come to Dunsinane.
DOCTOR, ⌜*aside*⌝
  Were I from Dunsinane away and clear,   75
  Profit again should hardly draw me here.
                                   They exit.

Scene 4

*Drum and Colors. Enter Malcolm, Siward, Macduff,
Siward's son, Menteith, Caithness, Angus, and Soldiers,
                        marching.*

MALCOLM
  Cousins, I hope the days are near at hand
  That chambers will be safe.

3. **nothing:** not at all
 7. **shadow:** conceal
 8. **host:** army; **discovery:** i.e., Macbeth's scouts
 11. **no other but:** nothing else **but** that
 12. **Keeps:** remains
 12–13. **endure . . . before 't:** not prevent our laying siege to it
 15. **where . . . given:** i.e., wherever opportunity offers itself
 16. **more and less:** nobles and commoners
 19–20. **Let . . . event:** i.e., **let** us wait to judge until we see the outcome **censures:** judgments **Attend:** await   **true event:** actual outcome
 26. **certain issue strokes must arbitrate:** i.e., the definite outcome **must** be decided by blows

A castle under siege, with scaling ladders. (5.5.1–3)
From [John Lydgate,] *The hystorye sege and dystruccyon of Troye* [1513].

MENTEITH   We doubt it nothing.
SIWARD
  What wood is this before us?
MENTEITH   The Wood of Birnam.
MALCOLM
  Let every soldier hew him down a bough
  And bear 't before him. Thereby shall we shadow
  The numbers of our host and make discovery
  Err in report of us.
SOLDIER   It shall be done.
SIWARD
  We learn no other but the confident tyrant
  Keeps still in Dunsinane and will endure
  Our setting down before 't.
MALCOLM   'Tis his main hope;
  For, where there is advantage to be given,
  Both more and less have given him the revolt,
  And none serve with him but constrainèd things
  Whose hearts are absent too.
MACDUFF   Let our just censures
  Attend the true event, and put we on
  Industrious soldiership.
SIWARD   The time approaches
  That will with due decision make us know
  What we shall say we have and what we owe.
  Thoughts speculative their unsure hopes relate,
  But certain issue strokes must arbitrate;
  Towards which, advance the war.
                        They exit marching.

5.5 Macbeth is confident that he can withstand any siege from Malcolm's forces. He is then told of Lady Macbeth's death and of the apparent movement of Birnam Wood toward Dunsinane Castle, where he waits. He desperately resolves to abandon the castle and give battle to Malcolm in the field.

---

4. **ague:** pestilence (pronounced *a-gue*)
5. **forced:** reinforced; also, perhaps, stuffed ("farced")
5–6. **those that should be ours:** i.e., deserters from our ranks
7. **met them:** i.e., in the field, in open battle; **dareful:** boldly
12. **my ... cooled:** I would have been chilled
13. **my fell of hair:** i.e., the hair on my scalp
14. **dismal treatise:** dreadful tale
15. **As:** as if
16. **Direness:** horror
17. **start:** startle
18. **Wherefore:** for what reason, why
20. **She should have died hereafter:** i.e., she would inevitably have died sometime; or, perhaps, she ought to have died at some future time
22–26. **Tomorrow ... death:** Behind Macbeth's terrible reflections lie the images of "life as a story" and "life as light." (See, e.g., Matthew 5.16.)
23. **petty:** slow, insignificant
24. **recorded time:** i.e., recordable **time**
26. **dusty death:** See Genesis 3.19: "for dust thou art, and unto dust shalt thou return."

Scene 5

Enter Macbeth, Seyton, and Soldiers, with Drum and Colors.

MACBETH
Hang out our banners on the outward walls.
The cry is still "They come!" Our castle's strength
Will laugh a siege to scorn. Here let them lie
Till famine and the ague eat them up.
Were they not forced with those that should be ours, 5
We might have met them dareful, beard to beard,
And beat them backward home.
                      A cry within of women.
                      What is that noise?

SEYTON
It is the cry of women, my good lord. ⌜*He exits.*⌝ 10
MACBETH
I have almost forgot the taste of fears.
The time has been my senses would have cooled
To hear a night-shriek, and my fell of hair
Would at a dismal treatise rouse and stir
As life were in 't. I have supped full with horrors. 15
Direness, familiar to my slaughterous thoughts,
Cannot once start me.

                      ⌜*Enter Seyton.*⌝

                      Wherefore was that cry?
SEYTON   The Queen, my lord, is dead.
MACBETH   She should have died hereafter. 20
There would have been a time for such a word.
Tomorrow and tomorrow and tomorrow
Creeps in this petty pace from day to day
To the last syllable of recorded time,
And all our yesterdays have lighted fools 25
The way to dusty death. Out, out, brief candle!

27. **shadow:** image without substance; also, actor; **player:** actor

38. **anon:** soon; **methought:** it seemed to me

46. **cling:** wither, shrink; **speech be sooth:** story is true

48. **pull in:** i.e., rein in; **resolution:** determination, steadfastness

49. **doubt:** suspect

54. **nor . . . nor:** neither . . . nor

56. **th' estate o' th' world:** perhaps, the settled order of the universe

57. **undone:** destroyed

A sixteenth-century image of Brutus's suicide. (5.8.1–2)
From Geoffrey Whitney, *A choice of emblemes* . . . (1586).

Life's but a walking shadow, a poor player
That struts and frets his hour upon the stage
And then is heard no more. It is a tale
Told by an idiot, full of sound and fury, 30
Signifying nothing.

Enter a Messenger.

Thou com'st to use thy tongue: thy story quickly.
MESSENGER   Gracious my lord,
I should report that which I say I saw,
But know not how to do 't. 35
MACBETH   Well, say, sir.
MESSENGER
As I did stand my watch upon the hill,
I looked toward Birnam, and anon methought
The Wood began to move.
MACBETH   Liar and slave! 40
MESSENGER
Let me endure your wrath if 't be not so.
Within this three mile may you see it coming.
I say, a moving grove.
MACBETH   If thou speak'st false,
Upon the next tree shall thou hang alive 45
Till famine cling thee. If thy speech be sooth,
I care not if thou dost for me as much.—
I pull in resolution and begin
To doubt th' equivocation of the fiend,
That lies like truth. "Fear not till Birnam Wood 50
Do come to Dunsinane," and now a wood
Comes toward Dunsinane.—Arm, arm, and out!—
If this which he avouches does appear,
There is nor flying hence nor tarrying here.
I 'gin to be aweary of the sun 55
And wish th' estate o' th' world were now
  undone.—

58. **alarum bell:** the **bell** that calls soldiers to arms; **wrack:** ruin, destruction
59. **harness:** i.e., armor

5.6 Malcolm arrives with his troops before Dunsinane Castle.

---

2. **uncle:** addressed to Siward
4. **battle:** battalion, main body; **we:** Note that Malcolm here uses the royal "we."
8. **Do we but:** i.e., if only we can; **power:** army
11. **harbingers:** announcers, forerunners

5.7 On the battlefield Macbeth kills young Siward, the son of the English commander. After Macbeth exits, Macduff arrives in search of him. Dunsinane Castle has already been surrendered to Malcolm, whose forces have been strengthened by deserters from Macbeth's army.

1-2. **They have ... course:** Macbeth here sees himself as a bear in a bearbaiting, tied **to a stake** and set upon by dogs. (See picture, page 182.) **course:** attack, encounter

Ring the alarum bell!—Blow wind, come wrack,
At least we'll die with harness on our back.
They exit.

Scene 6

Drum and Colors. Enter Malcolm, Siward, Macduff, and their army, with boughs.

MALCOLM
Now near enough. Your leafy screens throw down
And show like those you are.—You, worthy uncle,
Shall with my cousin, your right noble son,
Lead our first battle. Worthy Macduff and we
Shall take upon 's what else remains to do,   5
According to our order.
SIWARD   Fare you well.
Do we but find the tyrant's power tonight,
Let us be beaten if we cannot fight.
MACDUFF
Make all our trumpets speak; give them all breath,   10
Those clamorous harbingers of blood and death.
They exit.
Alarums continued.

Scene 7

Enter Macbeth.

MACBETH
They have tied me to a stake. I cannot fly,
But, bear-like, I must fight the course. What's he
That was not born of woman? Such a one
Am I to fear, or none.

Enter young Siward.

YOUNG SIWARD   What is thy name?   5

10. **title:** name
12. **fearful:** frightening, terrifying
14. **prove:** challenge, test
21. **still:** always
22. **kerns:** i.e., hired soldiers (more specifically, Irish foot soldiers)
23. **staves:** weapons; **Either thou:** i.e., **either** I find you
25. **undeeded:** i.e., unused
26–27. **one . . . bruited:** someone of great reputation is proclaimed
29. **gently rendered:** surrendered without a fight

Bearbaiting. (5.7.1; 5.8.34)
From [William Lily,] *Antibossicon* (1521).

MACBETH Thou'lt be afraid to hear it.
YOUNG SIWARD
  No, though thou call'st thyself a hotter name
  Than any is in hell.
MACBETH   My name's Macbeth.
YOUNG SIWARD
  The devil himself could not pronounce a title   10
  More hateful to mine ear.
MACBETH   No, nor more fearful.
YOUNG SIWARD
  Thou liest, abhorrèd tyrant. With my sword
  I'll prove the lie thou speak'st.
                    ⌜*They*⌝ *fight, and young Siward* ⌜*is*⌝ *slain.*
MACBETH   Thou wast born of   15
  woman.
  But swords I smile at, weapons laugh to scorn,
  Brandished by man that's of a woman born.
                                            He exits.

            Alarums. Enter Macduff.

MACDUFF
  That way the noise is. Tyrant, show thy face!
  If thou beest slain, and with no stroke of mine,   20
  My wife and children's ghosts will haunt me still.
  I cannot strike at wretched kerns, whose arms
  Are hired to bear their staves. Either thou, Macbeth,
  Or else my sword with an unbattered edge
  I sheathe again undeeded. There thou shouldst be;   25
  By this great clatter, one of greatest note
  Seems bruited. Let me find him, Fortune,
  And more I beg not.   *He exits. Alarums.*

        Enter Malcolm and Siward.

SIWARD
  This way, my lord. The castle's gently rendered.
  The tyrant's people on both sides do fight,   30

32. **itself professes:** announces itself
35. **strike beside us:** i.e., fight on our side, side by side

5.8 Macduff finds Macbeth, who is reluctant to fight with him because Macbeth has already killed Macduff's whole family and is sure of killing Macduff too if they fight. When Macduff announces that he is not, strictly speaking, a man born of woman, having been ripped prematurely from his mother's womb, then Macbeth is afraid to fight. He fights with Macduff only when Macduff threatens to capture him and display him as a public spectacle. Macduff kills Macbeth, cuts off his head, and brings it to Malcolm. With Macbeth dead, Malcolm is now king and gives new titles to his loyal supporters.

---

1. **Roman:** associated here with approval of suicide (See picture, page 178.)
2. **lives:** i.e., others living
6. **charged:** burdened
10. **Than terms can give thee out:** i.e., **than** words **can** describe you
12. **intrenchant:** invulnerable, unable to be cut
13. **impress:** leave a mark on
14. **crests:** heads
18. **angel:** i.e., evil spirit; **still:** always
20. **Untimely:** prematurely

The noble thanes do bravely in the war,
The day almost itself professes yours,
And little is to do.
MALCOLM   We have met with foes
That strike beside us.
SIWARD   Enter, sir, the castle.
                    They exit. Alarum.

⌜Scene 8⌝

Enter Macbeth.

MACBETH
Why should I play the Roman fool and die
On mine own sword? Whiles I see lives, the gashes
Do better upon them.

Enter Macduff.

MACDUFF   Turn, hellhound, turn!
MACBETH
Of all men else I have avoided thee.
But get thee back. My soul is too much charged
With blood of thine already.
MACDUFF   I have no words;
My voice is in my sword, thou bloodier villain
Than terms can give thee out.   *Fight. Alarum.*
MACBETH   Thou losest labor.
As easy mayst thou the intrenchant air
With thy keen sword impress as make me bleed.
Let fall thy blade on vulnerable crests;
I bear a charmèd life, which must not yield
To one of woman born.
MACDUFF   Despair thy charm,
And let the angel whom thou still hast served
Tell thee Macduff was from his mother's womb
Untimely ripped.

22. **my better part of man:** the greater **part of** my manhood (i.e., perhaps, courage)
23. **juggling:** deceiving
24. **palter . . . sense:** trick us by using words ambiguously
28. **show and gaze:** that which is gazed at; spectacle
30. **Painted upon a pole:** i.e., his picture **painted** and displayed on **a pole,** as for a sideshow; **underwrit:** written underneath
34. **baited:** attacked from all sides (as the bear is in a bearbaiting)
36. **opposed:** i.e., my opponent
38. **Lay on:** To **lay on** is to attack or assail vigorously.
39 SD. **They enter fighting, and Macbeth is slain:** This Folio stage direction is omitted by many editors because they feel that it contradicts the stage direction that immediately precedes it in the Folio: *"Exit fighting. Alarums."* Although early printed texts such as the Folio sometimes include duplicatory or contradictory stage directions, it is certainly possible in this case to perform all the directions printed in the Folio and reprinted here. **Retreat:** trumpet call signaling the retreat of a defeated army or the pulling back of a victorious army **flourish:** fanfare of trumpets or horns
40. **would:** wish; **miss:** lack
41. **go off:** i.e., die; **by these:** to judge by those present

MACBETH
Accursèd be that tongue that tells me so,
For it hath cowed my better part of man!
And be these juggling fiends no more believed
That palter with us in a double sense,
That keep the word of promise to our ear   25
And break it to our hope. I'll not fight with thee.
MACDUFF   Then yield thee, coward,
And live to be the show and gaze o' th' time.
We'll have thee, as our rarer monsters are,
Painted upon a pole, and underwrit   30
"Here may you see the tyrant."
MACBETH   I will not yield
To kiss the ground before young Malcolm's feet
And to be baited with the rabble's curse.
Though Birnam Wood be come to Dunsinane   35
And thou opposed, being of no woman born,
Yet I will try the last. Before my body
I throw my warlike shield. Lay on, Macduff,
And damned be him that first cries "Hold! Enough!"
They exit fighting. Alarums.

⌜*They*⌝ *enter fighting, and Macbeth* ⌜*is*⌝ *slain.* ⌜*Macduff
exits carrying off Macbeth's body.*⌝ *Retreat and flourish.
Enter, with Drum and Colors, Malcolm, Siward, Ross,
Thanes, and Soldiers.*

MALCOLM
I would the friends we miss were safe arrived.   40
SIWARD
Some must go off; and yet by these I see
So great a day as this is cheaply bought.
MALCOLM
Macduff is missing, and your noble son.
ROSS
Your son, my lord, has paid a soldier's debt.
He only lived but till he was a man,   45

46. **The which:** i.e., the fact that he had become **a man** (line 45)

47. **unshrinking station:** perhaps, unyielding stance; or, perhaps, steadfast refusal to give ground

53. **before:** on the front of his body

62. **score:** debt (the **soldier's debt** of line 44 and the death that one owes God or nature [Proverbial: "To pay one's debt to nature."])

67. **compassed ... pearl:** surrounded by the most choice subjects of your kingdom

73–74. **reckon ... even with you:** make an accounting of (also, take into account) the love each of you has shown, and discharge my debt to you

Fortune spinning her wheel. (5.7.27)
From Charles de Bouelles,
Que hoc volumine continentur [1510].

The which no sooner had his prowess confirmed
In the unshrinking station where he fought,
But like a man he died.
SIWARD Then he is dead?
ROSS
Ay, and brought off the field. Your cause of sorrow
Must not be measured by his worth, for then
It hath no end.
SIWARD Had he his hurts before?
ROSS
Ay, on the front.
SIWARD Why then, God's soldier be he!
Had I as many sons as I have hairs,
I would not wish them to a fairer death;
And so his knell is knolled.
MALCOLM
He's worth more sorrow, and that I'll spend for
   him.
SIWARD He's worth no more.
They say he parted well and paid his score,
And so, God be with him. Here comes newer
   comfort.

Enter Macduff with Macbeth's head.

MACDUFF
Hail, king! for so thou art. Behold where stands
Th' usurper's cursèd head. The time is free.
I see thee compassed with thy kingdom's pearl,
That speak my salutation in their minds,
Whose voices I desire aloud with mine.
Hail, King of Scotland!
ALL Hail, King of Scotland! *Flourish.*
MALCOLM
We shall not spend a large expense of time
Before we reckon with your several loves
And make us even with you. My thanes and
   kinsmen,

78. **Which ... time:** which should be done immediately in this new era
79. **As:** such **as**
81. **Producing ... ministers:** bringing forth (to justice) the agents
83. **self and violent hands:** her own **violent hands**

Henceforth be earls, the first that ever Scotland
In such an honor named. What's more to do,
Which would be planted newly with the time,
As calling home our exiled friends abroad
That fled the snares of watchful tyranny, 80
Producing forth the cruel ministers
Of this dead butcher and his fiend-like queen
(Who, as 'tis thought, by self and violent hands,
Took off her life)—this, and what needful else
That calls upon us, by the grace of grace, 85
We will perform in measure, time, and place.
So thanks to all at once and to each one,
Whom we invite to see us crowned at Scone.

Flourish. All exit.

Longer Notes

1.2.63. him: Editors disagree about whether the reference here is to the king of Norway or to the thane of Cawdor. A. R. Braunmuller, for instance (New Cambridge edition, 2008), argues that it must be Cawdor, since it describes him as "rebellious" ("rebellious arm 'gainst arm"), a term not really applicable to the king of Norway. While Braunmuller's is a valid point, we are nevertheless persuaded that the reference must be to Norway. G. L. Kittredge (*Macbeth*, in *Sixteen Plays of Shakespeare*, 1939) argues that Cawdor's treacherous assistance (lines 60–61) was done in secret and that the thane was therefore not at the battle. In support of this claim, we would note that Angus's speech at 1.3.116–24 stresses the fact that Cawdor's treachery was no open rebellion ("Whether he was combined [in conspiracy] / With those of Norway, or did line the rebel [i.e., reinforce Macdonwald] / With hidden help and vantage, or that with both / He labored in his country's wrack, I know not; / But treasons capital, confessed and proved, / Have overthrown him"). Further, had Macbeth fought "arm 'gainst arm" with Cawdor, it seems unlikely that he would, in 1.3, refer to Cawdor as "a prosperous gentleman" (line 76).

1.7.22. cherubin: Shakespeare elsewhere uses the words **cherubin** and *cherub* to refer to young winged angels, often depicted as infants with rosy, smiling faces (as in, for example, *Othello* 4.2.73, where Patience is called a "young and rose-lipped cherubin"). Here in Macbeth's speech, the reference seems primarily to be to the powerful supernatural winged creatures described in Ezekiel 1.5–14 (guardians of God's throne and representations of God's glory) and referred to in

Psalm 18.10, where God rides on a cherub when he comes to the rescue of the psalmist, David (". . . he rode upon a Cherub and did fly, and he came flying upon the wings of the wind").

2.3.8. **equivocator:** Equivocation was often associated with Jesuits, and many scholars see lines 2.3.7–11 as referring to the 1606 trial and execution for treason of Father Garnett, a Jesuit whose defense included his claim that by the doctrine of equivocation, a lie is not a lie if the speaker intends a second, true meaning by his words.

3.1.77 SD. **Murderers:** While the two men who enter here are called **murderers** in the Folio stage directions and speech prefixes, the dialogue in this scene suggests that the men are not yet **murderers,** but are instead desperate, poverty-stricken men who can thus be persuaded to kill for the king. The thrust of Macbeth's speeches to them is, first, that Banquo is the man responsible for their extreme poverty and that they would be cowards not to seek revenge on him, and, second, that Macbeth will reward them handsomely for the murder. The secondary meanings of such terms as **crossed** (line 88) and **instruments** (line 89) create a narrative in which the men have been **beggared** (line 101) by being dispossessed of their property by a greedy landowner (a process described and decried in many sixteenth-century writings); the men are now **reckless what** they **do** (lines 123–24) and are willing to undertake anything that will **mend** their lives (line 128). For Shakespeare's interest elsewhere in the problem of the social and economic creation of thieves and beggars, and for citations of early-sixteenth-century pleas on behalf of the dispossessed and starving, see Barbara A. Mowat, "Rogues, Shepherds, and the Counterfeit Distressed: Texts and Infracontexts of *The Winter's Tale* 4.3," *Shakespeare Studies* 23 (1994): 58–76, esp. pp. 66–69.

3.2.47. shard-born: Many editions (including our 1992 edition) follow the Folio in spelling this term "shard-borne" and gloss it as "borne on wings that are like shards (pieces of pottery)." Timothy Billings's essay "Squashing the 'shard-borne Beetle' Crux: A Hard Case with a Few Pat Readings" (*Shakespeare Quarterly* 56 [2005]: 434–47) demonstrates wittily (and definitively) that the traditional reading ("borne on shards") is indeed, as the *OED* notes, "due to misinterpretation of Shakes[peare]" (see *OED* "**shard-born, -borne**").

3.2.55. Cancel ... bond: The image presented in this line is that of a legal paper binding someone to pay a certain amount or to meet a certain obligation; such a **bond** can be canceled (rendered void by being crossed out or obliterated) or can be "[torn] to pieces," as Macbeth prays that it be. The context makes it clear that, figuratively, the **bond** somehow represents Banquo and his issue. Some editors think it possible that it could refer to Banquo himself, noting the echo of the language in Queen Margaret's prayer in *Richard III* (4.4.79) that God "Cancel his [Richard's] bond of life." (See, e.g., A. R. Braunmuller's New Cambridge edition.) Others see **bond** as referring to "the prophecy by which Fate has bound itself to give the throne to Banquo's descendants." (See, e.g., G. L. Kittredge.) Yet others interpret the **bond** more abstractly as "the bond of natural and moral law." (See Bevington, *Macbeth*, in *The Complete Works of Shakespeare*, 5th edition.) Thus, while the image of a legal document being destroyed (the vehicle of the metaphor) is clear, the tenor, the general sense of the line (Banquo and his issue being removed) is evident only from the context. Such resonant imprecision is characteristic of much of the language of this play, especially in the speeches of Macbeth, who seems to use such language to hide, while simultaneously revealing, his murderous thoughts.

3.4.41 SD. **Enter the Ghost:** While the ghost is not observed by Macbeth until line 54, this stage direction may, in fact, mark the ghost's actual, unobserved, entrance. On the other hand, the entrance is perhaps printed here in the Folio text because it reproduces a warning note in a playhouse manuscript reminding the prompter to alert the Banquo-actor to be ready to enter at around line 47 when "summoned" by Macbeth's "Were the graced person of our Banquo present."

Textual Notes

The reading of the present text appears to the left of the square bracket. The earliest sources of readings not in **F**, the First Folio text (upon which this edition is based), are indicated as follows: **F2** is the Second Folio of 1632; **F3** is the Third Folio of 1663–64; **F4** is the Fourth Folio of 1685; **Ed.** is an earlier editor of Shakespeare, beginning with Rowe in 1709. No sources are given for emendations of punctuation or for corrections of obvious typographical errors, like turned letters that produce no known word. **SD** means stage direction; **SP** means speech prefix; **uncorr.** means the first or uncorrected state of the First Folio; **corr.** means the second or corrected state of the First Folio; ~ stands in place of a word already quoted before the square bracket; ∧ indicates the omission of a punctuation mark.

1.1	10–11. SP SECOND WITCH ... THIRD WITCH] Ed.; *All* F
	10. calls.] ~∧ F
1.2	0. SD *King Duncan, Malcolm*] Ed.; *King Malcolme* F
	1 *and throughout play.* SP DUNCAN] Ed.; *King.* F
	15. gallowglasses] F2; Gallowgrosses F
	16. quarrel] Ed.; Quarry F
	28. break] Ed.; *omit* F
1.3	40. Forres] Ed.; Soris F
	100. make,] ~∧ F
	102. Came] Ed.; Can F
1.4	1. Are] F2; Or F
1.5	1 *and throughout play.* SP LADY MACBETH] Ed.; *Lady.* F
	37–38. him, ... preparation?] ~? ... ~. F

	74.	matters. To . . . time,] ~, ~ . . . ~. F
1.6	5.	martlet] Ed.; Barlet F
	6.	mansionry] Ed.; Mansonry F
	7.	jutty,] ~∧ F
	10.	most] Ed.; must F
	37.	host.] ~∧ F
1.7	5.	end-all∧] ~∧ ~. F
	6.	shoal] Ed.; Schoole F
	47–49.	esteem, . . . adage?] ~? . . . ~. F
	52.	do] Ed.; no F
	81–82.	officers, . . . quell?] ~? . . . ~. F
2.1	67.	strides] Ed.; sides F
	69.	sure] Ed.; sowre F
	70.	way they] Ed.; they may F
2.2	17.	SD *after line 11 in* F
	93.	SD *after "deed" in* F
2.3	0.	SD *Knocking within. Enter a Porter.*] Ed.; *Enter a Porter. Knocking within.* F
	20.	SD *The . . . Lennox.*] This ed.; *Enter Macduff, and Lenox.* F *1 line later*
	44.	SD *1 line earlier in* F
	84.	SD *1 line later in* F
	159.	SD *All . . . exit.*] Ed.; *Exeunt.* F
2.4	52.	Well,] ~∧ F
3.1	10.	SD *Lady Macbeth, Lennox*] Ed.; *Lady Lenox* F
	45–46.	night. . . . welcome,] ~, . . . ~: F
	81, 131, 159.	SP MURDERERS] Ed.; *Murth.* F
	118.	heart∧] ~; F
	162.	SD *He exits.*] Ed.; *Exeunt.* F
3.3	9.	and] F2; end F
3.4	10.	thanks.] ~∧ F
	94.	time] Ed.; times F
	144.	worse.] ~∧ F
	167.	worst.] ~, F
	176.	in deed] F (indeed)

Textual Notes

3.6 28. son] Ed.; Sonnes F
42. the] Ed.; their F
50. t' hold] F2; t hold F
4.1   5. throw.] ~∧ F
38. SD *to*] Ed.; *and* F
62. germens . . . all together] Ed.; Germaine, . . . altogether F
83. thanks.] ~∧ F
94. assurance∧] ~: F
107. SD *He descends.*] Ed.; *Descend.* F
120. SD *1 line later in* F
126. SD *A . . . last.*] This ed.; *A shew of eight Kings, and Banquo last, with a glasse in his hand.* F
134. eighth] F (eight)
4.2   1 *and throughout scene.* SP LADY MACDUFF] Ed.; *Wife* F
75. ones!] ~∧ F
76. thus∧] ~. F
87. SD *1 line later in* F
89 *and throughout scene.* SP MURDERER] Ed.; *Mur.* F
98. SD *Lady . . . body.*] Ed.; *Exit crying Murther.* F
4.3   5. downfall'n] Ed.; downfall F
18. deserve] Ed.; discerne F
33–35. child, . . . leave-taking?] ~? . . . ~-~. F
43. affeered] F (affear'd)
125. accursed] F2; accust F
142. detraction,] ~. F
146. own,] ~. F
152. thy] F2; they F
152. here-approach] Ed.; ~∧ ~ F
166. SD *1 line earlier in* F
176. on with] F *corr.;* on my with F *uncorr.*
183. not] F2; nor F

	199.	relation∧] ~; F
	251.	SP ROSS] F *corr.;* Roffe. F *uncorr.*
	273.	myself.] ~∧ F
	276.	tune] Ed.; time F
5.1	39–41.	fear∧ ... account?] ~? ... ~. F
5.3	25.	disseat] Ed.; dis-eate F
	49.	her] F2; *omit* F
	64.	pristine] F2; pristiue F
5.4	10.	SP SOLDIER] Ed.; *Sold.* F
5.5	8.	SD *1 line later in* F
	44.	false] F2; fhlse F

Macbeth:
A Modern Perspective

Susan Snyder

Coleridge pronounced *Macbeth* to be "wholly tragic." Rejecting the drunken Porter of Act 2, scene 3 as "an interpolation of the actors," and perceiving no wordplay in the rest of the text (he was wrong on both counts), he declared that the play had no comic admixture at all. More acutely, though still in support of this sense of the play as unadulterated tragedy, he noted the absence in *Macbeth* of a process characteristic of other Shakespearean tragedies, the "reasonings of equivocal morality."[1]

Indeed, as Macbeth ponders his decisive tragic act of killing the king, he is not deceived about its moral nature. To kill anyone to whom he is tied by obligations of social and political loyalty as well as kinship is, he knows, deeply wrong:

> He's here in double trust:
> First, as I am his kinsman and his subject,
> Strong both against the deed; then, as his host,
> Who should against his murderer shut the door,
> Not bear the knife myself.   (1.7.12–16)

And to kill Duncan, who has been "so clear in his great office" (that is, so free from corruption as a ruler), is to compound the iniquity. In adapting the story of Macbeth from Holinshed's *Chronicles of Scotland*, Shakespeare created a stark black-white moral opposition by omitting from his story Duncan's weakness as a monarch while retaining his gentle, virtuous nature. Unlike his prototype in Holinshed's history, Macbeth kills not an ineffective leader but a saint whose benevolent presence blesses Scotland. In the same vein of polarized morality, Shakespeare departs from the Holinshed account in which Macbeth is joined in regicide by Banquo and others; instead, he has Macbeth act alone against Duncan. While it might be good politics to distance Banquo from guilt (he was an ancestor of James I, the current king of England and patron of Shakespeare's acting company), excluding the other thanes as well suggests that the playwright had decided to focus on private, purely moral issues uncomplicated by the gray shades of political expediency.

Duncan has done nothing, then, to deserve violent death. Unlike such tragic heroes as Brutus and Othello, who are enmeshed in "equivocal morality," Macbeth cannot justify his actions by the perceived misdeeds of his victim. "I have no spur," he admits, "To prick the sides of my intent, but only / Vaulting ambition" (1.7.25–27). This ambition is portrayed indirectly rather than directly. But it is surely no accident that the Weïrd Sisters accost him and crystallize his secret thoughts of the crown into objective possibility just when he has hit new heights of success captaining Duncan's armies and defeating Duncan's enemies. The element of displacement and substitution here—Macbeth leading the fight for Scotland while the titular leader waits behind the lines for the outcome—reinforces our sense that, whatever mysterious timetable the Sisters work by, this is the psychologically right moment to confront Macbeth with their predictions of greatness. Hailed as thane of Glamis, thane of Cawdor, and king, he is initially curious and disbelieving. Though his first fearful reaction (1.3.54) is left unexplained, for us to fill in as we will, surely one way to read his fear is that the word "king" touches a buried nerve of desire. When Ross and Angus immediately arrive to announce that Macbeth is now Cawdor as well as Glamis, the balance of skepticism tilts precipitously toward belief. The nerve vibrates intensely. Two-thirds of the prophecy is already accomplished. The remaining prediction, "king hereafter," is suddenly isolated and highlighted; and because of the Sisters' now proven powers of foreknowledge, it seems to call out for its parallel, inevitable fulfillment.

The Weïrd Sisters present nouns rather than verbs. They put titles on Macbeth without telling what actions he must carry out to attain those titles. It is Lady Macbeth who supplies the verbs. Understanding that her husband is torn between the now-articulated object of desire and the fearful deed that must achieve it ("wouldst not play false / And yet wouldst wrongly win," 1.5.22–23), she persuades him by harping relentlessly on manly *action*. That very gap between noun and verb, the desired prize and the doing necessary to win it, becomes a way of taunting him as a coward: "Art thou afeard / To be the same in thine own act and valor / As thou art in desire?" (1.7.43–45). A man is one who closes this gap by strong action, by taking what he wants; whatever inhibits that action is unmanly fear. And a man is one who does what he has sworn to do, no matter what. We never see Macbeth vow to kill Duncan, but in Lady Macbeth's mind just his broaching the subject has become a commitment. With graphic horror she fantasizes how she would tear her nursing baby from her breast and dash its brains out if she had sworn as she says her husband did. She would, that is, violate her deepest nature as a woman and sever violently the closest tie of kinship and dependence. Till now, Macbeth has resisted such violation, clinging to a more humane definition of "man" that accepts fidelity and obligation as necessary limits on his prowess. Now, in danger of being bested by his wife in this contest of fierce determinations, he accepts her simpler, more primitive equation of manhood with killing: he commits himself to destroying Duncan. It is significant for the lack of "equivocal morality" that even Lady Macbeth in this crucial scene of persuasion doesn't try to manipulate or blur the polarized moral scheme. Adopting instead a warrior ethic apart from social morality, she presents the murder not as good but as heroic.

Moral clarity informs not only the decisions and actions of *Macbeth* but the stage of nature on which they are played out. The natural universe revealed in the play is essentially attuned to the good, so that it reacts to the unambiguously evil act of killing Duncan with disruptions that are equally easy to read. There are wild winds, an earthquake, "strange screams of death" (2.3.61–69). And beyond such general upheaval there is a series of unnatural acts that distortedly mirror Macbeth's. Duncan's horses overthrow natural order and devour each other, like Macbeth turning on his king and cousin. "A falcon, tow'ring in her pride of place"— the monarch of birds at its highest pitch—is killed by a mousing owl, a lesser bird who ordinarily preys on insignificant creatures (2.4.15–16). Most ominous of all, on the morning following the king's death, is the absence of the sun: like the falcon a symbol of monarchy, but expanding that to suggest the source of all life. In a general sense, the sunless day shows the heavens "troubled with man's act" (2.4.7), but the following grim metaphor points to a closer and more sinister connection: "dark night strangles the traveling lamp" (2.4.9). The daylight has been murdered like Duncan. Scotland's moral darkness lasts till the end of Macbeth's reign. The major scenes take place at night or in the atmosphere of the "black, and midnight hags" (4.1.48), and there is no mention of light or sunshine except in England (4.3.1).

Later in the play, nature finds equally fitting forms for its revenge against Macbeth. Despite his violations

A Modern Perspective   205

of the natural order, he nevertheless expects the laws of nature to work for him in the usual way. But the next victim, Banquo, though his murderer has left him "safe in a ditch" (3.4.28), refuses to stay safely still and out of sight. In Macbeth's horrified response to this restless corpse, we may hear not only panic but outrage at the breakdown of the laws of motion:

> The time has been
> That, when the brains were out, the man would die,
> And there an end. But now they rise again
> With twenty mortal murders on their crowns
> And push us from our stools. This is more strange
> Than such a murder is.   (3.4.94–99)

His word choice is odd: "*they* rise," a plural where we would expect "he rises," and the loaded word "crowns" for heads. Macbeth seems to be haunted by his last victim, King Duncan, as well as the present one. And by his outraged comparison at the end—the violent death and the ghostly appearance compete in strangeness—Macbeth suggests, without consciously intending to, that Banquo's walking in death answers to, or even is caused by, the murder that cut him off so prematurely. The unnatural murder generates unnatural movement in the dead. Lady Macbeth, too, walks when she should be immobile in sleep, "a great perturbation in nature" (5.1.10).

It is through this same ironic trust in natural law that Macbeth draws strength from the Sisters' later prophecy: if he is safe until Birnam Wood come to Dunsinane, he must be safe forever:

> Who can impress the forest, bid the tree
> Unfix his earthbound root? Sweet bodements, good!
> Rebellious dead, rise never till the Wood
> Of Birnam rise . . .   (4.1.109–12)

His security is ironic because for Macbeth, of all people, there can be no dependence on predictable natural processes. The "rebellious dead" have already unnaturally risen once; fixed trees can move against him as well. And so, in time, they do. Outraged nature keeps matching the Macbeths' transgressions, undoing and expelling their perversities with its own.

In tragedies where right and wrong are rendered problematic, the dramatic focus is likely to be on the complications of choice. *Macbeth,* on the contrary, is preoccupied less with the protagonist's initial choice of a relatively unambiguous wrong action than with the moral decline that follows. H. B. Charlton noted that one could see in *Richard III* as well as *Macbeth* the biblical axiom that "the wages of sin is death"; but where the history play *assumes* the principle, *Macbeth* demonstrates why it has to be that way.[2] The necessity is not so much theological as psychological: we watch in Macbeth the hardening and distortion that follows on self-violation. The need to suppress part of himself in order to kill Duncan becomes a refusal to acknowledge his deed ("I am afraid to think what I have done. / Look on 't again I dare not": 2.2.66–67). His later murders are all done by proxy, in an attempt to create still more distance between the destruction he wills and full psychic awareness of his responsibility. At the same time, murder becomes a necessary activity, the verb now a compulsion almost without regard to the object: plotted after he has seen the Weïrd Sisters' apparitions, Macbeth's attack on Macduff's "line" (4.1.174) is an insane double displacement, of fear of Macduff himself and fury at the vision of the line of kings fathered by Banquo.

Yet the moral universe of *Macbeth* is not as uncomplicated as some critics have imagined. To see in the play's human and physical nature only a straightforward pattern of sin and punishment is to gloss over the questions it raises obliquely, the moral complexities and mysteries it opens up. The Weïrd Sisters, for example, remain undefined. Where do they come from? Where do they go when they disappear from the action in Act 4? What is their place in a moral universe that ostensibly recoils against sin and punishes it? Are they human witches, or supernatural beings? Labeling them "evil" seems not so much incorrect as inadequate. Do they cause men to commit crimes, or do they only present the possibility to them? Macbeth responds to his prophecy by killing his king, but Banquo after hearing the one directed at him is not impelled to act at all. Do we take this difference as demonstrating that the Sisters have in themselves no power beyond suggestion? Or should we rather find it somewhat sinister later on when Banquo, ancestor of James I or not, sees reason in Macbeth's success to look forward to his own—yet feels it necessary to conceal his hopes (3.1.1–10)?

Even what we most take for granted becomes problematic when scrutinized. Does Macbeth really desire to be king? Lady Macbeth says he does, but what comes through in 1.5 and 1.7 is more her desire than his. Apart from one brief reference to ambition when he is ruling out other motives to kill Duncan, Macbeth himself is strangely silent about any longing for royal power and position. Instead of an obsession that fills his personal horizon, we find in Macbeth something of a motivational void. Why does he feel obligated, or compelled, to bring about an advance in station that the prophecy seems to render inevitable anyway? A. C. Bradley put his finger on this absence of positive desire when he observed that Macbeth commits his crime as if it were "an appalling duty."[3]

Recent lines of critical inquiry also call old certainties into question. Duncan's saintly status would seem assured, yet sociological critics are disquieted by the way we are introduced to him, as he receives news of the battle in 1.2. On the one hand we hear reports of horrifying savagery in the fighting, savagery in which the loyal thanes participate as much as the rebels and invaders—more so, in fact, when Macbeth and Banquo are likened to the crucifiers of Christ ("or memorize another Golgotha," 1.2.44). In response we see Duncan exulting not only in the victory but in the bloodshed, equating honor with wounds. It is not that he bears any particular guilt. Yet the mild paternal king is nevertheless implicated here in his society's violent warrior ethic, its predicating of manly worth on prowess in killing.[4] But isn't this just what we condemn in Lady Macbeth? Cultural analysis tends to blur the sharp demarcations, even between two such figures apparently totally opposed, and to draw them together as participants in and products of the same constellation of social values.

Lady Macbeth and Duncan meet in a more particular way, positioned as they are on the same side of Scotland's basic division between warriors and those protected by warriors. The king is too old and fragile to fight; the lady is neither, but she is barred from battle by traditional gender conventions that assign her instead the functions of following her husband's commands and nurturing her young. In fact, of course, Lady Macbeth's actions and outlook thoroughly subvert this ideology, as she forcefully takes the lead in planning the murder and shames her husband into joining in by her willingness to slaughter her own nurseling. It is easy to call Lady Macbeth "evil," but the label tends to close down analysis exactly where we ought to probe more deeply. Macbeth's wife is restless in a social role that in spite of her formidable courage and energy offers no chance of independent action and heroic achievement.

It is almost inevitable that she turn to achievement at second hand, through and for her husband. Standing perforce on the sidelines, like Duncan once again, she promotes and cheers the killing.

Other situations, too, may be more complex than at first they seem. Lady Macduff, unlike Lady Macbeth, accepts her womanly function of caring for her children and her nonwarrior status of being protected. But she is not protected. The ideology of gender seems just as destructive from the submissive side as from the rebellious, when Macduff deserts her in order to pursue his political cause against Macbeth in England and there is no husband to stand in the way of the murderers sent by Macbeth. The obedient wife dies, with her cherished son, just as the rebellious, murderous lady will die who consigned her own nursing baby to death. The moral universe of *Macbeth* has room for massive injustice. Traditional critics find Lady Macbeth "unnatural," and even those who do not accept the equation of gender ideology with nature can agree with the condemnation in view of her determined suppression of all bonds of human sympathy. Clear enough. But we get more blurring and crossovers when Macduff's wife calls *him* unnatural. In leaving his family defenseless in Macbeth's dangerous Scotland, he too seems to discount human bonds. His own wife complains bitterly that "he wants the natural touch"; where even the tiny wren will fight for her young against the owl, his flight seems to signify fear rather than natural love (4.2.8–16). Ross's reply, "cruel are the times," while it doesn't console Lady Macduff and certainly doesn't save her, strives to relocate the moral ambiguity of Macduff's conduct in the situation created by Macbeth's tyrannical rule. The very political crisis that pulls Macduff away from his family on public business puts his private life in jeopardy through the same act of desertion. But while acknowledging the peculiar tensions raised by a tyrant-king, we may also see in the Macduff family's disaster a tragic version of a more familiar conflict: the contest between public and private commitments that can rack conventional marriages, with the wife confined to a private role while the husband is supposed to balance obligations in both spheres.

Malcolm is allied with Duncan by lineage and with Macduff by their shared role of redemptive champion in the final movement of the play. He, too, is not allowed to travel through the action unsullied. After a long absence from the scene following the murder of Duncan, he reappears in England to be sought by Macduff in the crusade against Macbeth. Malcolm is cautious and reserved, and when he does start speaking more freely, what we hear is an astonishing catalogue of self-accusations. He calls himself lustful, avaricious, guilty of every crime and totally lacking in kingly virtues:

> Nay, had I power, I should
> Pour the sweet milk of concord into hell,
> Uproar the universal peace, confound
> All unity on earth.   (4.3.113–16)

Before people became so familiar with Shakespeare's play, I suspect many audiences believed what Malcolm says of himself. Students on first reading still do. Why shouldn't they? He has been absent from the stage for some time, and his only significant action in the early part of the play was to run away after his father's murder. When this essentially unknown prince lists his vices in lengthy speeches of self-loathing, there is no indication—except an exaggeration easily ascribable to his youth—that he is not sincere. And if we do believe, we cannot help joining in Macduff's distress.

A Modern Perspective

Malcolm, the last hope for redeeming Scotland from the tyrant, has let us down. Duncan's son is more corrupt than Macbeth. He even sounds like Macbeth, whose own milk of human kindness (1.5.17) was curdled by his wife; who threatened to destroy the whole natural order, "though the treasure / Of nature's germens tumble all together / Even till destruction sicken" (4.1.60–63). In due course, Malcolm takes it all back; but his words once spoken cannot simply be canceled, erased as if they were on paper. We have already, on hearing them, mentally and emotionally processed the false "facts," absorbed them experientially. Perhaps they continue to color indirectly our sense of the next king of Scotland.

Viewed through various lenses, then, the black and white of *Macbeth* may fade toward shades of gray. The play is an open system, offering some fixed markers with which to take one's basic bearings but also, in closer scrutiny, offering provocative questions and moral ambiguities.

---

1. "Notes for a Lecture on *Macbeth*" [c. 1813], in *Coleridge's Writings on Shakespeare*, ed. Terence Hawkes (New York: Capricorn, 1959), p. 188.

2. H. B. Charlton, *Shakespearian Tragedy* (Cambridge: Cambridge University Press, 1948), p. 141.

3. A. C. Bradley, *Shakespearean Tragedy* (London: Macmillan, 1904), p. 358.

4. James L. Calderwood, *If It Were Done: "Macbeth" and Tragic Action* (Amherst: University of Massachusetts Press, 1986), pp. 77–89.

Further Reading

Macbeth

Adelman, Janet. " 'Born of Woman': Fantasies of Maternal Power in *Macbeth*." In *Cannibals, Witches, and Divorce: Estranging the Renaissance*, edited by Marjorie Garber, pp. 90–121. Baltimore: Johns Hopkins University Press, 1987.

Focusing on Macbeth's repeated question, "What's he / That was not born of woman?" Adelman argues that *Macbeth* simultaneously represents the fantasy of absolute, destructive maternal power and the male fantasy of absolute escape from this power. Only through the ruthless elimination of all female presence are the primitive fears of male identity ultimately assuaged and contained. Initially the witches, with their prophecy that Macbeth fulfills, and Lady Macbeth, impelling him to murder by her equation of masculinity and regicide, appear to wield great power over him as their pawn, and the play's images of masculinity and femininity are terribly disturbed. While Duncan combines attributes of the father and the mother in harmonious relation, male and female break apart with his assassination, the female becoming either helpless or poisonous, the male bloodthirsty. There is the suggestion that Duncan has failed to provide protective masculine authority. This father-king cannot shield either his vulnerable female self or his sons from the violence provoked in Macbeth by the maternal malevolence of the witches and Lady Macbeth, who are identified with each other. "Through this identification, Shakespeare in effect locates the source of his culture's fear of witchcraft in individual human history, in the infant's long dependence on female figures felt as all-powerful: what the witches suggest about the vulnerability of men to female power on the cosmic plane, Lady Macbeth doubles on the psychological plane." Adelman then charts the declining power of the witches as the play enters its fourth act, when we discover they have masters and they become less terrifying and more comic. They have only ever been English witches, Adelman observes, and not the more menacing Continental witches associated with "the ritual murder and eating of infants, the attacks specifically on the male genitals, the perverse sexual relationship with demons." Such threatening features are instead transferred to Lady Macbeth in her relationship to Macbeth, who comes to imagine "her as male and then reconstitutes himself as the invulnerable male child of such a mother." While the play punishes Macbeth for his fantasy of absolute escape from maternal power, it nonetheless "curiously enacts the fantasy that it seems to deny," specifically in the figure of Macduff: "in affirming that Macduff has indeed had a mother, [the play] denies the fantasy of male self-generation; but in attributing his power to his having been untimely ripped from that mother, it sustains the sense that violent separation from the mother is the mark of the successful male."

Bradley, A. C. *Shakespearean Tragedy: Lectures on Hamlet, Othello, King Lear, Macbeth.* 1904. Reprint, London: St. Martin's Press, 1985.

Bradley finds *Macbeth* simpler than Shakespeare's other tragedies, "broader and more massive in effect." "The whole tragedy is sublime." He focuses on the psychological makeup of Macbeth and Lady Macbeth, finding that Duncan's murder is a moment of radical change in the protagonists' characters. With his emphasis on psychology, Bradley is concerned to make Macbeth entirely free of any coercion by the witches, leaving him responsible for Duncan's murder and those that follow: "Shakespeare nowhere shows ... any interest in the speculative problems of foreknowledge, predestination and freedom." The witches are neither "fate, whom Macbeth is powerless to resist," nor "symbolic representations of the ... half-conscious guilt of Macbeth." According to Bradley, Macbeth is "a great warrior, somewhat masterful, rough, and abrupt," but with the imagination of a poet—an imagination through which conscience works to affect him with horror at evil. "But he has never ... accepted as the principle of his conduct the morality which takes shape in his imaginative fears." The instant he murders Duncan, the futility of his act "is revealed to Macbeth as clearly as its vileness had been revealed beforehand." There ensues a "perpetual agony of restlessness ... which urges him to causeless action in search of oblivion." Yet "there remains something sublime in the defiance with which, even when cheated of his last hope, he faces earth and hell and heaven." Lady Macbeth is initially characterized by "an inflexibility of will, which appears to hold imagination, feeling, and conscience completely in check." She is appalling and sublime, apparently invincible but also apparently inhuman. "We find no trace of pity ... ; no consciousness of the treachery and baseness of the murder; ... no shrinking even from the condemnation or hatred of the world." However, she is shocked by the hideousness of Duncan's murder when she sees it reflected, upon its discovery, in the faces of others, and "her nature begins to sink." She loses the initiative—"the stem of her being seems to be cut through"—while the opposite occurs with her husband, who "comes into the foreground."

Brown, John Russell. *Macbeth*. Shakespeare Handbooks. New York: Palgrave Macmillan, 2005.

Brown's handbook devotes chapters to the play's date of composition and textual provenance, a scene-by-scene commentary, cultural contexts and sources, and the afterlife of *Macbeth* in the theater, on film, and in criticism. Brown thinks that the play was probably written and first performed late in 1606 or early the following year; he reprints Dr. Simon Forman's diary account of a revival at the Globe on April 20, 1611, the earliest documented performance of the play. Public interest in witchcraft during the early years of the century, changing views toward Scotland, challenges to royal absolutism, debates about the qualities required for a good monarch, and interest stirred by the Gunpowder Plot trial early in 1606 are all part of the play's cultural context. While Shakespeare borrows from the Bible and Book of Common Prayer (see, for example, the Porter episode in 2.3, which reflects "Christian beliefs and superstitions more specifically than elsewhere" in the play), his primary source was Holinshed's *Chronicles of England, Scotland and Ireland* (extensively excerpted by Brown in order to reveal Shakespeare's choices). The author speculates that Shakespeare might have approved additions to the original text—e.g., songs taken from Middleton's *The Witch* and two entries for Hecate in 3.5 and 4.1.38 SD–43—even if he did not actually write them. The text's "unusual brevity could also be a consequence of a revision that had to accommodate additional singing, dancing and spectacle for performances at court or Blackfriars." The eighty-page commentary, informed by textual issues and theatrical concerns, demonstrates how the dialogue, at crucial moments in the plot, "repeatedly quickens the senses and frees the imagination of those who speak and those who hear," and how Shakespeare's handling of the onstage action "repeatedly directs attention to innermost thoughts and physical sensations." The chapter on key productions and performances includes discussion of William Davenant's staging (late 1660s) and the performances of David Garrick and Sarah Siddons (eighteenth century), Henry Irving and Ellen Terry (nineteenth century), Laurence Olivier and Vivian Leigh (1955), Ian McKellen and Judi Dench in Trevor Nunn's Royal Shakespeare Company production (1976), and Antony Sher and Harriet Walter in Gregory Doran's revival for the same company (1999) and for the Young Vic (London, 2000). Adaptations singled out for comment include Charles Marowitz's *A Macbeth* (1969), Eugène Ionesco's *Macbeth* (1972), Tom Stoppard's *Dogg's Hamlet, Cahoot's Macbeth* (1979), Welcome Msomi's frequently revived *Umabatha* (1970), and a well-received Japanese version by Yukio Ninagawa (1980) that enjoyed a re-production in 1998. The chapter on cinematic treatments considers three films: Akira Kurosawa's "masterpiece," *Throne of Blood* (1957); Roman Polanski's *Macbeth* (1971); and Trevor Nunn's 1978 video version of his 1976 staging noted above. In the final chapter, Brown examines a selected number of critical views (most dating from the 1950s on) under the headings of verbal language, characters, arguments and themes, structure and genre, and theatrical events in the play's afterlife. A briefly annotated bibliography rounds out the volume.

Calderwood, James L. *If It Were Done: "Macbeth" and Tragic Action.* Amherst, Mass.: University of Massachusetts Press, 1986.

 Calderwood addresses *Macbeth* from three different—but not entirely discrete—perspectives. First, he argues for the play's indebtedness to *Hamlet*, not because of similarities but because the two tragedies are almost systematically opposed; *Macbeth* is the "photographic negative of *Hamlet*" or the "counter-*Hamlet*." Hamlet's words are opposed to Macbeth's action. *Hamlet* is full of "pre-action," the revenge not coming until the end, while in *Macbeth* the regicide comes early and its consequences linger on. Hamlet appears to sleep in inaction for most of his play; Macbeth, having killed Duncan, can sleep no more. "In *Hamlet* the middle—the interim, the gap, the space between two persons or events—is always clogged.... *Macbeth* features an increasingly easy erasure of inbetweenness in the interests of immediacy." Second, Calderwood discusses the play as a tragedy "about the nature of tragedy," finding *Macbeth* to deviate relentlessly from the Aristotelian observation that tragedy is an imitation of an action that is whole and complete in itself, with a beginning that does not follow from something else, a middle, and an end from which nothing follows. *Macbeth* "does not begin where it seems to begin because its action has already begun," as the Weïrd Sisters in its first scene are waiting until "the hurly-burly's done" and "the battle" between Duncan's forces and the rebels has been "lost and won." Furthermore, the end of *Macbeth* so closely resembles its beginning that we are left to wonder how its action can be complete: at the beginning Macbeth wins a battle to secure Duncan on the throne, and at the end Macduff wins another battle to install Malcolm on the throne. *Macbeth* also appears incomplete because Shakespeare does not stage the play's central action, the murder of Duncan, and because Macbeth himself does not understand his murder of Duncan to be the completion of necessary action, but has to supplement that murder with the murders of Banquo (itself left incomplete by the escape of Fleance) and of Macduff's wife and family (that crime left unfinished by Macbeth's failure to kill Macduff). Third, Calderwood questions "the assumption that Macbeth's evil can be sharply divided from the prevailing Scots good." He observes that the narration of the play's opening battle presents "Scots culture as founded on savagery" insofar as it figures Macbeth and Banquo "as priestly leaders of the royal forces . . . [who] preside over a ceremony in which the Scots are purged and exalted by the shedding of sacred blood in the king's cause." Therefore, while in murdering Duncan, "Macbeth violates basic cultural tabus, . . . his deed issues . . . from an impulse to transcend bestiality and achieve cultural distinction" through violence, which the play has represented as the means through which the distinction is made between king and subject in Scotland. Finally, the play seems to move toward a ritual as it ends with the violent invasion of Scotland to "terminate violence by purging the country of the *pharmakos*," the scapegoat, Macbeth. However, tragedy cannot be reduced to ritual: "we witness a divided Macbeth, a tyrant yet one who acknowledges repellence in himself as well as in the world outside him." As his enemies view him as "merely a 'cursed usurper,' a 'butcher,' . . . in some measure Macbeth shares their judgment [and] he transcends their judgment. It is the destiny of tragic heroes to be isolated in self-division and nuance, as the world they have violated returns to an oblivious but healing wholeness."

Charlton, H. B. "*Macbeth.*" In *Shakespearian Tragedy*, pp. 141–88. Cambridge: Cambridge University Press, 1948.

For Charlton, "*Macbeth* explores imaginatively and dramatically the operations of the human conscience as it worked in a spiritual epoch before it had been precisely named." Macbeth's conscience is "mainly a feeling of fear," and evil in *Macbeth* is "unnaturalness rather than unrighteousness. . . . The afterworld remains mistily beyond the edges of the known, and exerts no pressure on the minds and the feelings of living men." The measure of human worth is "unswerving courage against greatest odds," and Macbeth is only vaguely aware that other conditions limit the scope within which bravery may properly act. Among these conditions are the obligations of "kinship, of loyalty, and of hostship," as well as the desire to be worthy of the tribute of fame. Macbeth's conscience operates as much through his corporeal as his spiritual agencies, his fear of violating natural obligations registering itself in the breakdown of harmony in his "state of man": "The hand is incapable of performing the willed movement; the eye distorts the image it perceives; the very hair erects itself unseasonably; the blood flushes or leaves pale the face, unsubjected to a controlling will.... Imagination intensifies the fear inordinately until function is smothered in enervating surmise." Even as Macbeth becomes habituated to murder, he is incapable of destroying his human nature, which, as it endures the accumulating unnaturalness of his action, only increases his sensitivity and spiritual awareness. "Through Macbeth, man appears to be discovering human nature and the principles or laws which are its very essence. In the end, these laws emerge as something not hostile to, but as it were, precedent to all and every formulation of them in terms of religious dogma.... Macbeth appears to stand as the symbol of a crucial moment in human history, the moment at which mankind discovered itself to be possessed of capacities for entering on unending vistas of spiritual progress."

Coleridge, S. T. "Notes for a Lecture on *Macbeth*" [c. 1813]. In *Coleridge's Writings on Shakespeare*, edited by Terence Hawkes, pp. 188–99. New York: Capricorn, 1959.

Despising 2.3.1–43 (with the character of the Porter), Coleridge focuses on the Weïrd Sisters, Macbeth, Lady Macbeth, and Banquo. He offers to generalize the principles underlying the characters of Macbeth and Lady Macbeth: "Macbeth mistranslates the recoilings and ominous whispers of conscience into prudential and selfish reasonings, and after the deed, the terrors of remorse into fear from external dangers—like delirious men that run away from the phantoms of their own brain, or, raised by terror to rage, stab the real object that is within their own reach; while Lady Macbeth merely endeavours to reconcile him and her own sinkings of heart by anticipation of the worst shapes and thoughts, and affected bravado in confronting them." Coleridge describes a Macbeth who "is powerful in all things but [who] has strength in none. Morally he is *selfish*; *i.e.*, as far as his weakness will permit him to be. Could he have everything he wanted, he would *rather* have it innocently.... Lady Macbeth... is... of high rank, left much alone, and feeding herself with day-dreams of ambition, she mistakes the courage of fantasy for the power of bearing the consequences of the realties of guilt. Hers is the mock fortitude of a mind deluded with ambition; she shames her husband with a super-human audacity of fancy which she cannot support, but sinks in the season of remorse, and dies in suicidal agony." It is the first appearance of the Weïrd Sisters that establishes the "keynote of the character of the whole play." Coleridge sets the powerful invocation of the imagination in this scene in contrast to the comparatively mundane opening of *Hamlet*. He goes on to contrast the openness with which Banquo responds to the Weïrd Sisters with Macbeth's brooding melancholy, concluding that Macbeth has already been tempted by ambitious thoughts.

Garber, Marjorie. "Macbeth: The Male Medusa." In *Shakespeare's Ghost Writers: Literature as Uncanny Causality*, pp. 116–65. New York: Routledge, 2010.

Sigmund Freud famously denied any relation between the literary appearance of ghosts or apparitions and the *Unheimlich*, or uncanny. In response Garber argues that *Macbeth*, with its witches, ghost, and apparitions, "is *the* play of the uncanny—the uncanniest in the canon"—and that "the uncanny is nothing less than the thematized subtext of" the play, which is about the transgression of boundaries and about dislocation, "something let out to wander," like the sleepwalking Lady Macbeth or the ghost of Banquo at the banquet. The essay begins with a review of the stage traditions surrounding *Macbeth*, particularly the prohibition against using the name *Macbeth* in the theater outside of performance. The play itself stages the revelation of that which is not to be looked upon in, for example, what the French poet Stéphane Mallarmé calls "a seemingly fortuitous violation" through which we see the witches prematurely at the beginning of the play, or later in what Macduff, unexpectedly finding Duncan murdered, calls "a new Gorgon," one of the feminized mythological monsters the sight of which turned the observer to stone. Macduff's mythological allusion becomes the occasion in Garber's essay for a wide-ranging exploration of the Gorgon Medusa's significance in classical and Renaissance art and literature, with each significance related to *Macbeth*. Garber canvasses the Italian mythographer Caesare Ripa, the English Francis Bacon, the Scottish James I in his book *Basilikon Doron*, and even the archaeological remains of Roman Britain that include many images of the female Medusa and some of a male one. From *Macbeth* Garber produces a seemingly endless list of manifestations of the uncanny: "the witches' riddling prophecies, the puzzling, spectacular apparitions, the walking of trees and sleepers, the persistent sense of doubling that pervades the whole play: two Thanes of Cawdor; two kings and two kingdoms, England and Scotland themselves doubled and divided; two heirs apparent to Duncan; the recurrent prefix 'Mac' itself which means 'son of'; the sexually ambiguous witches replicated in the willfully unsexed Lady Macbeth."

Harris, Jonathan Gil. "The Smell of *Macbeth*." *Shakespeare Quarterly* 58 (2007): 465–86. The original essay is incorporated into Harris, *Untimely Matter in the Time of Shakespeare,* chapter 4, "The Smell of Gunpowder: *Macbeth* and the Palimpsests of Olfaction" (pp. 119–39) (Philadelphia: University of Pennsylvania Press, 2009).

Arguing that the smell of "thunder and lightning" at the beginning of *Macbeth* is as theatrically significant as its acoustic power, Harris widens the usual auditory and visual emphasis of historical phenomenological studies to include the olfactory. With Proust's repeated allusions to smell and memory as a reference point, Harris "locate[s] in smell . . . a polychronicity: that is, a palimpsesting of diverse moments in time." The author's polychronic reading of *Macbeth*'s "smellscape" reveals "an explosive temporality through which the past can be made to act upon, and shatter the self-identity of, the present." The malodorous smell of gunpowder and fireworks used in the seventeenth century to create the "fog and filthy air" and the illusion of thunder and lightning in the first scene would have entailed for the playgoer "a palimpsesting of temporally discrete events and conventions: the contemporary Gunpowder Plot, the older stage tradition of firework-throwing devils and Vices, and the abandoned sacred time of Catholic ritual in which fair and foul smells [of burning incense] signified, respectively, divine and satanic presence." Each of these memories would have rendered the play's pyrotechnics "untimely" in the sense of being transformed "into something else, something unstuck in [or out of] time." The stink emitted by the detonated squib allowed "a supposedly superseded religious past to intervene in and pluralize the Protestant present." Harris concludes that a polychronic approach to the "time-traveling" associations of smell in *Macbeth* makes us more sensitive to "the extent to which the vagaries of matter, time, and memory on the Shakespearean stage ... demand special, and necessarily incomplete, practices of interpretation."

Hawkins, Michael. "History, Politics, and *Macbeth*." In *Focus on Macbeth*, edited by John Russell Brown, pp. 155–88. London: Routledge & Kegan Paul, 1982.

Examining political questions that concerned Shakespeare's contemporaries, Hawkins discusses how these debates are dealt with in *Macbeth*. He finds *Macbeth* treating four issues in particular: (1) Macbeth's taking decisive action, commended as likely to bring success in the midst of political uncertainty; (2) Macbeth as a "free agent," the witches notwithstanding; (3) Macbeth as having the political advantage over his opponents in that he knows the future; and (4) Macbeth as successful when following the prophecies, "unsuccessful when he tries to thwart them." Hawkins goes on to consider Shakespeare's exploration of political concerns in three coexisting phases of politics in *Macbeth*: the prefeudal, characterized by blood and kinship relations; the feudal, in which personal obligations extend beyond kinship relations to include outsiders; and the postfeudal, with the role of king greatly enhanced. Relevant to the prefeudal phase is the murder of Duncan *as a kinsman* that gives rise to the "classic solution of the blood feud," with Duncan and Malcolm avenged on Macbeth through their agent Macduff, who is also avenging the murder of his own family. Also associated with prefeudal politics, for Hawkins, are "the dangers of wifely domination and uxoriousness and the hollowness of childlessness," although, argues Hawkins, it is precisely because Macbeth is childless that the blood feud ends with his death.

Feudal politics are manifest in the play through the "existence of a thanely class, supposedly possessed of the chivalric virtues of personal courage, loyalty, and honour." In debate within feudal politics are manliness (in the sense of personal courage) and its relation to ambition, as opposed to loyalty. While Macbeth questions his wife's absolute relation of manliness to violence, nonetheless the beginning and the end of the play present such a relation in Macbeth's feats of war and Macduff's attack on him. Feudal politics also characterize personal courage as arising from "the admired virtues of love of greatness, magnanimity, and desire for fame," all forms of ambition that may be a threat to loyalty. Finally, in terms of postfeudal politics centered on monarchy, *Macbeth* explores the legitimacy of the monarch, the extent to which his judgment (poor in Duncan's case) is subject to the review of his subjects, and the extent to which they enjoy the right to resist, especially through violence. These topics arise in the play not only from Macbeth's assassination of Duncan but also from the invasion of Scotland later by a largely English army to seat Malcolm on the throne.

Leggatt, Alexander. "*Macbeth*: A Deed without a Name." In Leggatt, *Shakespeare's Tragedies: Violation and Identity*, chapter 7 (pp. 177–204). Cambridge: Cambridge University Press, 2005.

Central to Leggatt's examination of the intertwined themes of violation and identity in Shakespeare's tragedies is the idea that just as the actor playing a role is and is not the character, so a "character is and is not so and so." This "doubleness" in the character's identity "links with the doubleness of the act of atrocity that breaks him/her," the violation "becom[ing] figuratively connected with other acts, including acts of love" (e.g., Romeo and Juliet's first sexual encounter and the shedding of Tybalt's blood). As the idea of violation pervades not only the individual character violated but that character's other relationships, "relationship itself comes into question." In *Macbeth*, the murder of Duncan, an act even its perpetrators find difficult to name, haunts the play, taking on a life of its own. With echoes of Doomsday permeating the scene of discovery (2.3.89–92, 94, and 148), the regicide "become[s] the essence of all crime, and crime itself, in a breakdown of meaning, infiltrates the idea of judgment." Emphasizing the importance of Macbeth and Lady Macbeth as a couple, Leggatt reads the violation of Duncan as a "displaced sexual act" that "consummate[s] their marriage." Although the marital relationship begins to unravel in the aftermath of the murder, the couple's reaching out to each other in Act 5, when each is most alone, shows that the bond firmly established in the initial scenes is not completely destroyed. Although physically absent, Macbeth is the addressee in the "one-sided conversation" of his wife's sleepwalking sequence (5.1); similarly, Lady Macbeth, though dead, pervades all of the ideas expressed in the "Tomorrow and tomorrow and tomorrow" speech (5.5.22–31). In these scenes, both Macbeth and Lady Macbeth, after struggling throughout the play to deny their humanity, exemplify "the human bond" in a way that continues to haunt readers and audiences alike. The final section of the chapter takes up the unsettled nature of the play's ending: i.e., the troubling absence of Donalbain, the "inhuman stoicism" of Siward, the unreassuring echo of the Witches in the repeated cries of "Hail" (5.8.65, 70, and 71), and the chilling virginity of Malcolm. What appears on the surface to be a loud public play, beginning and ending with the sounds and sights of battle, "has at its still, frightening center a murder in a domestic space, and turns out on closer inspection to be one of Shakespeare's most intimate dramas, his fullest examination of a marriage," one "sealed in blood."

McEachern, Claire. "The Englishness of the Scottish Play: *Macbeth* and the Poetics of Jacobean Union." In *The Stuart Kingdoms in the Seventeenth Century: Awkward Neighbors*, edited by Allan I. Macinnes and Jane Ohlmeyer, pp. 94–112. Portland, Ore.: Four Courts Press, 2002.

Responding to the doubleness often identified as the play's signature quality, McEachern reads *Macbeth*'s "refractive vision" as one of national identity; "its source, that of a newly Jacobean England's sense of cultural difference." With the 1603 accession of James VI of Scotland to the throne of England as James I, England's awkward neighbor to the north, once "alien and ... other," was now "admirable ... and self." As England "begins to be imagined not as an exclusively self-determining property" (the elect nation and sole occupant of the island celebrated in John of Gaunt's "sceptered isle" tribute [*Richard II* 2.1.45]), she finds herself entering into a new relationship that requires a new national perspective. In the Elizabethan period, a distinguishing marker of Scottish versus English thinking was Scotland's inclusive rather than exclusive concern with boundaries. McEachern underscores this distinction in describing the idea of Scotland at that time as custodial, rooted in "fierce kin-bonds," while that of England was monarchal, embodied in a chaste and royally resistant authority that emphasizes the alliance of monarchy with exclusion. When James became King of England, however, the monarch's body was no longer one of "exclusion but of forceful inclusion."

McEachern concentrates on four scenes near the end of *Macbeth* (4.3 through 5.3) to argue that the tragedy "comprehends that of Elizabethan patriotism itself." Malcolm and the Scottish rebels, in their fight against Macbeth's tyranny (5.2), seek "an infusion of English manhood to supply the loss of Scotland's own," something "gracious England" is ready to supply (4.3.53–54); Macbeth, on the other hand, as he fights for a Scotland defined by "images of bounded security" (5.5.2–8), targets his anger not only at the rebels but even more at the invading "English epicures" (5.3.9). Whereas Malcolm mirrors Scottish inclusion in his first royal act, the naming of former thanes as earls (5.8.74–77), Macbeth reflects English exclusivity in his fierce drive to preserve the purity of Scotland's borders. The disassociated mind and body of the sleepwalking Lady Macbeth, the cut branches of Birnam Wood, and the decapitated head of Macbeth all figure "the severing of a language of nationhood from its original roots." In short, Shakespeare uses the "death of a Scottish patriot . . . [to make] us feel the loss of a thoroughly English nation."

Moschovakis, Nick, ed. *Macbeth: New Critical Essays*. Shakespeare Criticism Series 32. New York: Routledge, 2008.

The editor opens this anthology with a "discursive bibliographic essay," organized around the "shifting relationship [over four centuries] between two conflicting strains" in the play's critical and theatrical reception: the "dualistic" *Macbeth*, which "assures us . . . that we can tell 'good' from 'evil,'" versus the "problematic"

Macbeth, which "throw[s] doubt on our ability to distinguish" the two, thereby "substantiating the weird sisters' contention that 'Fair is foul, and foul is fair' (1.1.12)." The majority of the seventeen essays that follow the introduction focus on the discourses of politics, class, gender, the emotions, and the economy: Rebecca Lemon, "Sovereignty and Treason in *Macbeth*"; Jonathan Baldo, "'A rooted sorrow': Scotland's Unusable Past"; Rebecca Ann Bach, "The 'Peerless' Macbeth: Friendship and Family in *Macbeth*"; Julie Barmazel, "'The servant to defect': Macbeth, Impotence, and the Body Politic"; Abraham Stoll, "*Macbeth*'s Equivocal Conscience"; Lois Feuer, "Hired for Mischief: The Masterless Man in *Macbeth*"; Stephen Deng, "Healing Angels and 'Golden Blood': Money and Mystical Kingship in *Macbeth*"; Lisa A. Tomaszewski, "'Throw physic to the dogs!': Moral Physicians and Medical Malpractice in *Macbeth*"; and Lynne Dickson Bruckner, "'Let grief convert to anger': Authority and Affect in *Macbeth*." Two essays consider topics in performance theory: Michael David Fox, "Like a Poor Player: Audience Emotional Response, Nonrepresentational Performance, and the Staging of Suffering in *Macbeth*"; and James Wells, "'To be thus is nothing': *Macbeth* and the Trials of Dramatic Identity." Other selections deal with particular productions and adaptations: Laura Engel's analysis of Sarah Siddons's Lady Macbeth, Stephen M. Buhler's examination of Barbara Garson's *MacBird* and Seth Greenland's *Jungle Rot*, BI-QI Beatrice Lei's look at *Macbeth* in Chinese opera, Kim Fedderson and J. Michael Richardson's account of recent "migrations of the cinematic brand," and Bruno Lessard's exploration of "hypermedia *Macbeth*." In the final essay, "Sunshine in *Macbeth*," Pamela Mason "offers perspectives on the First Folio text, its handling by modern editors, and the relationship between text and performance."

Newstok, Scott L., and Ayanna Thompson, eds. *Weyward Macbeth: Intersections of Race and Performance*. New York: Palgrave Macmillan, 2010.

The Newstok and Thompson anthology of twenty-six new essays provides an interdisciplinary approach to "the various ways *Macbeth* has been adapted and appropriated within the context of American racial constructions." In the introductory essay "What is a 'Weyward' *Macbeth*?" Ayanna Thompson defines "weyward" as "weird, fated, fateful, perverse, intractable, willful, erratic, unlicensed, fugitive, troublesome, and wayward." Such semantic diversity (mirroring the typographical "multiplicity *and* instability" of the Folio's "weyward" and "weyard") makes it "precisely the correct word for *Macbeth*'s role in American racial formations." A companion essay by Celia R. Daileader ("Weird Brothers: What Thomas Middleton's *The Witch* Can Tell Us about Race, Sex, and Gender in *Macbeth*") tackles the "weyward" qualities of the playtext itself. The next five essays (grouped under the heading "Early American Intersections") explore how debates about freedom, slavery, and racial/national identity haunt nineteenth- and early twentieth-century treatments of the Scottish play: Heather S. Nathans, "'Blood will have blood': Violence, Slavery, and *Macbeth* in the Antebellum American Imagination"; John C. Briggs, "The Exorcism of Macbeth: Frederick Douglass's Appropriation of Shakespeare"; Bernth Lindfors, "Ira Aldridge as Macbeth"; Joyce Green MacDonald, "Minstrel Show *Macbeth*"; and Nick Moschovakis, "Reading *Macbeth* in Texts by and about African Americans, 1903–44: Race and the Problematics of Allusive Identification." Section Three, titled "Federal Theatre Project(s)," includes Lisa N. Simmons, "Before Welles: A 1935 Boston Production"; Marguerite Rippy, "Black Cast Conjures White Genius: Unraveling the Mystique of Orson Welles's 'Voodoo'

Macbeth"; Scott L. Newstok, "After Welles: Re-do Voodoo *Macbeth*s"; and Lenwood Sloan, "The Vo-Du *Macbeth!*: Travels and Travails of a Choreo-Drama Inspired by the FTP Production." Moving to early twenty-first-century stagings, Section Four "provide[s] ... snapshots of five distinctly racialized adaptations of *Macbeth*": Harry J. Lennix, "A Black Actor's Guide to the Scottish Play, or, Why *Macbeth* Matters"; Alexander C. Y. Huang, "Asian-American Theatre Reimagined: Shogun *Macbeth* in New York"; Anita Maynard-Losh, "The Tlingit Play: *Macbeth* and Native Americanism"; José A. Esquea, "A Post-Apocalyptic *Macbeth*: Teatro LA TEA's *Macbeth* 2029"; and William C. Carroll, "Multicultural, Multilingual *Macbeth*." The essays in the remaining three sections address "different facets of *Macbeth*'s allusive force in music, film, and drama": Wallace McClain Cheatham, "Reflections on Verdi, *Macbeth*, and Non-Traditional Casting in Opera"; Douglas Lanier, "Ellington's Dark Lady"; Todd Landon Barnes, "Hip-Hop *Macbeth*s, 'Digitized Blackness,' and the Millennial Minstrel: Illegal Culture Sharing in the Virtual Classroom"; Francesca Royster, "Riddling Whiteness, Riddling Certainty: Roman Polanski's *Macbeth*"; Courtney Lehmann, "Semper Die: Marines Incarnadine in Nina Menkes's *The Bloody Child: An Interior of Violence*"; Amy Scott-Douglass, "Shades of Shakespeare: Colorblind Casting and Interracial Couples in *Macbeth in Manhattan, Grey's Anatomy*, and Prison *Macbeth*"; Charita Gainey-O'Toole and Elizabeth Alexander, "Three Weyward Sisters: African-American Female Poets Conjure with *Macbeth*"; Philip C. Kolin, " 'Black up again': Combating *Macbeth* in Contemporary African-American Plays"; and Peter Erickson, "Black Characters in Search of an Author: Black Plays on Black Performers of Shakespeare." Richard Burt's epilogue, "Oba Macbeth: National Transition as National Traumission," considers "the weyward nature of historical transmission" in the context of the "current socio-political moment: the presidency of Barack Hussein Obama." An appendix on selected productions of *Macbeth* featuring nontraditional casting rounds out the volume.

Norbrook, David. "*Macbeth* and the Politics of Historiography." In *Politics of Discourse: The Literature and History of Seventeenth-Century England*, edited by Kevin Sharpe and Steven N. Zwicker, pp. 78–116. Berkeley: University of California Press, 1987.

Norbrook separates himself from the practitioners of cultural materialism and new historicism prominent in the 1980s. Of the cultural-materialist readings of Shakespeare's plays, he writes that "The very plays that a generation ago were acclaimed as bastions of traditional values in a declining world are now seen as radically subverting all values and authority." Of the new-historicist readings, he says that "when this [cultural-materialist] approach seems inadequate, it may be argued that this [new-historicist] subversion in fact subtly reinforced the very power structures that were being challenged." Norbrook is uncomfortable with both approaches because "they effectively reduplicate the stark oppositions presented by absolutist propagandists: either monarchy or anarchy." To situate *Macbeth* in the context of the political debates of its own time, Norbrook draws extensively on histories of Scotland that include accounts of Macbeth's rule written in the sixteenth century by such highly educated and politically engaged humanist historians as John Major, Hector Boece, and George Buchanan, all of whom had "studied at the Sorbonne [in Paris] when it was a center of radical political thought." Norbrook locates in the work of these historians of Scotland radical political theories. For example, Buchanan argued that kings were to be chosen by their nobles and could reign only at the pleasure of their nobles, who had the right to overthrow and even kill kings corrupted by power. According to Norbrook, Shakespeare, who "took a sophisticated political interest in Scottish history," revised the radicalism found in these historical accounts; nonetheless, *Macbeth* engages with such accounts "in a subtle, oblique, carefully weighed manner, rather than through violent reaction." Some anomalies and contradictions in the play arise from difficulties in their source material; an example is the play's ambivalence about whether the throne of Scotland is inherited through patrilineal descent or is awarded through election by the nobles—an issue often in dispute in Scottish history. All in all, for Norbrook, "Macbeth was a figure bound to evoke ambivalent responses from a Renaissance humanist. If the audience can sympathize with Macbeth even though he outrages the play's moral order, it may be because vestiges remain of a worldview in which regicide could be a noble rather than an evil act."

Sinfield, Alan. "*Macbeth*: History, Ideology and Intellectuals." *Critical Quarterly* 28 (1986): 63–77.

Sinfield sets out to disturb the conventional reading of *Macbeth* by arguing that it is grounded in certain distinctions that are called into question by the play itself. The first such distinction is between allegedly legitimate violence used in the service of the State (such as Macbeth's "unseaming" the rebel Macdonwald "from the nave [i.e., navel] to the chops [i.e., jaws]" on the battlefield) and so-called illegitimate violence against the State (such as Macbeth's assassination of Duncan). The play, though, according to Sinfield, breaks down this distinction by presenting the violence used against Macbeth's State as legitimate. A second distinction postulated by the conventional reading of the play is between a monarch whose claim to the throne is legitimate and whose rule is therefore just (Duncan) and a tyrant who usurps the throne and goes on to oppress his people (Macbeth). Again, according to Sinfield, the play does not maintain this distinction consistently, for it appears to have Macbeth both enjoy proper election to the monarchy by the thanes and nonetheless tyrannize Scotland. Sinfield traces the conventional reading of the play to writing by James I of England and VI of Scotland, particularly his *The Trew Law of Free Monarchies*, and finds a historical basis for questioning these views in the writing of George Buchanan, whose published works on Scottish history James sought to suppress.

Stallybrass, Peter. "*Macbeth* and Witchcraft." In *Focus on Macbeth*, edited by John Russell Brown, pp. 189–209. London: Routledge & Kegan Paul, 1982.

Viewing witchcraft in *Macbeth* as an expression of a dominantly patriarchal society, Stallybrass describes both the actual Renaissance beliefs about witches and "the *function* of such beliefs." One Renaissance belief is that witches are opposed to monarchy: witches "might kill the king or forecast the hour of his death or seek to know who would succeed the living monarch." The belief in such an antithesis between monarchy and witchcraft had as its corollary the following: "If kingship is legitimated by analogy to God's rule over the earth, and the father's rule over the family and the head's rule over the body, witchcraft establishes the opposite analogies, whereby the Devil attempts to rule over the earth, and the woman over the family, and the body over the head." *Macbeth* gathers up in its representation of witches a wide range of beliefs about them, associating witches (and therefore Macbeth, who seeks to preserve his connection to them) with the grand (disorders in nature, prophecy) and the inconsequential (familiars—Graymalkin and Paddock—"withered" old women, petty vendettas, swine-killing). Lady Macbeth is shown to practice witchcraft when she invokes the overthrow of nature within herself. Yet in the latter half of the play witchcraft is shown to fail: in the sleepwalking scene, for example, Lady Macbeth is reduced by the return of "the compunctious visitations of nature," and the witches themselves become the agents who present the providential future of Scotland's monarchy—the witches now reduced to what was their antithesis.

Before Stallybrass attempts to generalize about the function of witchcraft in *Macbeth*, he also canvasses the representation of witchcraft in the most notorious Continental scholarly work on the subject, Krämer and Sprenger's *Malleus Maleficarum* (1486), and in anthropological writing on social functions of witchcraft in Ghana and Nupe. In these cases and in *Macbeth*, he concludes, the sociological function of witchcraft is the confirmation of the prevailing patriarchal ideology through the repression of women by means of moving the debate about gender hierarchy to "the undisputed ground of 'Nature,'" in, for example, as noted above, *Macbeth*'s sleepwalking scene. Stallybrass resists critical attempts to find in *Macbeth* any historically or politically transcendent meaning.

Wheeler, Richard. "'Since first we were dissevered': Trust and Autonomy in Shakespearean Tragedy and Romance." In *Representing Shakespeare: New Psychoanalytical Essays*, edited by Murray M. Schwartz and Coppélia Kahn, pp. 170–87. Baltimore: Johns Hopkins University Press, 1980.

Wheeler's goal is "to identify polarized trends in Shakespeare's development, separated by generic distinctions in the earlier work [e.g., comedies, histories], which confront each other in the drama of the tragic period," which represent "modes of seeking self-fulfillment in conditions of extreme crisis." At one extreme, "a deeply feared longing for merger subverts relations of trust; at the other, failed autonomy gives way to helpless isolation," as in *Macbeth*. "Macbeth's desperate reliance on the will of his powerful wife" is a relation of unqualified trust, which ultimately proves destructive as he experiences "absolute aloneness" or "empty isolation... bereft even of desire for relations with others." "The quest for royal manhood in *Macbeth* requires that Macbeth's ambition be nurtured into action by others. After the first exchange with the witches, Macbeth is driven to achieve a magically compelling ideal of manhood articulated for him by his wife. Macbeth cannot refuse this ideal, but he cannot pursue it except by making himself a child to the demonic motherhood held out to him by Lady Macbeth." Wheeler continues by noting that "As the merger of the two characters dissolves, Macbeth's sustained violence, always exercised in the context of family relations—a fatherly king [Duncan], a father and son [Banquo and Fleance], and finally a mother and her 'babes' [Lady Macduff and her children]—only serves to isolate him further, until even the illusion of omnipotence nurtured by the witches collapses before the force of a man 'not born of woman,'" Macduff. Wheeler thereby relates Shakespearean tragedy, including *Macbeth*, to accounts of early childhood development, like those of Margaret Mahler, who tells us that "As the ego develops along the boundaries that distinguish the world from the self, crises in the process of separation [from the mother] can engender the wish to reinhabit the symbiotic unity of infant and mother; crises within the environment provided by the mother, including those that provoke fears of 'reengulfment,' can lead to the defiant repudiation of essential others and to fantasies of a powerful autonomous self that magically incorporates symbiotic omnipotence."

Wilder, Lina Perkins. " 'Flaws and Starts': Fragmented Recollection in *Macbeth.*" In Wilder, *Shakespeare's Memory Theatre: Recollection, Properties, and Character,* chapter 6 (pp. 156–70). Cambridge: Cambridge University Press, 2010.

Wilder's study of Shakespeare's use of mnemonic objects to "help audiences recall, or imagine, staged and unstaged pasts" examines how "props, the players, and the physical space of the stage provide the vocabulary of Shakespeare's memory theatre." Central to this materialist-cognitive reading of *Macbeth* is the role of Lady Macbeth as a "memory pedagogue": in the first part of the play, she instructs her husband in the "masculine discipline" of forgetting; in the banquet scene, as his "sweet remembrancer" (3.4.42), she reminds him of his duties as host, thereby functioning as a "human . . . memento who shapes and directs his remembering in ways that reinforce social stability." Probing the pathological nature of the fragmentary memories that "punctuate" the play, Wilder argues that neither Lady Macbeth's recollection of having given suck nor Macbeth's of the witches' enigmatic prophecies embodies a "fully imagined past"; on the contrary, both cases exemplify "a memory culture in which masculine control and deliberate forgetting have become the norm." The play's chief irony is that she who urged her husband not to "be governed by undisciplined, uncontrolled remembrance" is in the end "entirely constituted by and finally destroyed by uncontrolled remembering." The sleepwalking scene (5.1), which Wilder discusses at some length as the "ultimate expression" of "simultaneous recollection and invention," not only "construct[s in part] an unstaged past" but also "recalls the entire play in single words" (e.g., the recurring "ones" and "twos," "time," "do," and "it"). In the course of the chapter, the author examines such "mnemonically charged" devices as the absent child of Lady Macbeth's early discourse (the violence done to the sucking babe [1.7.62–66] reverberating in Macduff's declaration of his violent cesarean birth at 5.8.19–20), the "absent prop" of blood specified in the dialogue following the offstage murder but not in the stage directions of 2.2, the onstage "banquet" that recalls the name of the dead man who haunts Macbeth in 3.4, the evocative images conjured by the witches in 4.1 (which, taken together, make the remainder of the play "an explicitly mnemonic form as each further catastrophe recalls an element of the prophecy"), and the letters referred to by the Gentlewoman in 5.1.4–9, whose contents remain tantalizingly inaccessible. Wilder concludes that unlike the "narrative elaboration and rhetorical mastery" marking the recollections of characters in other plays by Shakespeare (e.g., Othello and Iago), recollection in *Macbeth*—a play in which "the past shatters"—"never quite becomes narrative."

Shakespeare's Language

Abbott, E. A. *A Shakespearian Grammar*. New York: Haskell House, 1972.

This compact reference book, first published in 1870, helps with many difficulties in Shakespeare's language. It systematically accounts for a host of differences between Shakespeare's usage and sentence structure, and our own.

Blake, Norman. *Shakespeare's Language: An Introduction*. New York: St. Martin's Press, 1983.

This general introduction to Elizabethan English discusses various aspects of the language of Shakespeare and his contemporaries, offering possible meanings for hundreds of ambiguous constructions.

Dobson, E. J. *English Pronunciation, 1500–1700.* 2 vols. Oxford: Clarendon Press, 1968.

This long and technical work includes chapters on spelling (and its reformation), phonetics, stressed vowels, and consonants in early modern English.

Hope, Jonathan. *Shakespeare's Grammar.* London: Arden Shakespeare, 2003.

Commissioned as a replacement for Abbott's *Shakespearian Grammar*, Hope's book is organized in terms of the two basic parts of speech, the noun and the verb. After extensive analysis of the noun phrase and the verb phrase come briefer discussions of subjects and agents, objects, complements, and adverbials.

Houston, John. *Shakespearean Sentences: A Study in Style and Syntax.* Baton Rouge: Louisiana State University Press, 1988.

Houston studies Shakespeare's stylistic choices, considering matters such as sentence length and the relative positions of subject, verb, and direct object. Examining plays throughout the canon in a roughly chronological, developmental order, he analyzes how sentence structure is used in setting tone, in characterization, and for other dramatic purposes.

Onions, C. T. *A Shakespeare Glossary.* Oxford: Clarendon Press, 1986.

This revised edition updates Onions's standard, selective glossary of words and phrases in Shakespeare's plays that are now obsolete, archaic, or obscure.

Robinson, Randal. *Unlocking Shakespeare's Language: Help for the Teacher and Student.* Urbana, Ill.: National Council of Teachers of English and the ERIC Clearinghouse on Reading and Communication Skills, 1989.

Specifically designed for the high-school and undergraduate college teacher and student, Robinson's book addresses the problems that most often hinder present-day readers of Shakespeare. Through work with his own students, Robinson found that many readers today are particularly puzzled by such stylistic characteristics as subject-verb inversion, interrupted structures, and compression. He shows how our own colloquial language contains comparable structures, and thus helps students recognize such structures when they find them in Shakespeare's plays. This book supplies worksheets—with examples from major plays—to illuminate and remedy such problems as unusual sequences of words and the separation of related parts of sentences.

Williams, Gordon. *A Dictionary of Sexual Language and Imagery in Shakespearean and Stuart Literature.* 3 vols. London: Athlone Press, 1994.

Williams provides a comprehensive list of words to which Shakespeare, his contemporaries, and later Stuart writers gave sexual meanings. He supports his identification of these meanings by extensive quotations.

Shakespeare's Life

Baldwin, T. W. *William Shakspere's Petty School.* Urbana: University of Illinois Press, 1943.

Baldwin here investigates the theory and practice of the petty school, the first level of education in Elizabethan England. He focuses on that educational system primarily as it is reflected in Shakespeare's art.

Further Reading 241

Baldwin, T. W. *William Shakspere's Small Latine and Lesse Greeke*. 2 vols. Urbana: University of Illinois Press, 1944.

Baldwin attacks the view that Shakespeare was an uneducated genius—a view that had been dominant among Shakespeareans since the eighteenth century. Instead, Baldwin shows, the educational system of Shakespeare's time would have given the playwright a strong background in the classics, and there is much in the plays that shows how Shakespeare benefited from such an education.

Beier, A. L., and Roger Finlay, eds. *London 1500-1700: The Making of the Metropolis*. New York: Longman, 1986.

Focusing on the economic and social history of early modern London, these collected essays probe aspects of metropolitan life, including "Population and Disease," "Commerce and Manufacture," and "Society and Change."

Bentley, G. E. *Shakespeare's Life: A Biographical Handbook*. New Haven: Yale University Press, 1961.

This "just-the-facts" account presents the surviving documents of Shakespeare's life against an Elizabethan background.

Chambers, E. K. *William Shakespeare: A Study of Facts and Problems*. 2 vols. Oxford: Clarendon Press, 1930.

Analyzing in great detail the scant historical data, Chambers's complex, scholarly study considers the nature of the texts in which Shakespeare's work is preserved.

Cressy, David. *Education in Tudor and Stuart England*. London: Edward Arnold, 1975.

This volume collects sixteenth-, seventeenth-, and

early eighteenth-century documents detailing aspects of formal education in England, such as the curriculum, the control and organization of education, and the education of women.

Dutton, Richard. *William Shakespeare: A Literary Life*. New York: St. Martin's Press, 1989.

Not a biography in the traditional sense, Dutton's very readable work nevertheless "follows the contours of Shakespeare's life" as he examines Shakespeare's career as playwright and poet, with consideration of his patrons, theatrical associations, and audience.

Honan, Park. *Shakespeare: A Life*. New York: Oxford University Press, 1998.

Honan's accessible biography focuses on the various contexts of Shakespeare's life—physical, social, political, and cultural—to place the dramatist within a lucidly described world. The biography includes detailed examinations of, for example, Stratford schooling, theatrical politics of 1590s London, and the careers of Shakespeare's associates. The author draws on a wealth of established knowledge and on interesting new research into local records and documents; he also engages in speculation about, for example, the possibilities that Shakespeare was a tutor in a Catholic household in the north of England in the 1580s and that he acted particular roles in his own plays, areas that reflect new, but unproven and debatable, data—though Honan is usually careful to note where a particular narrative "has not been capable of proof or disproof."

Schoenbaum, S. *William Shakespeare: A Compact Documentary Life*. New York: Oxford University Press, 1977.

This standard biography economically presents the essential documents from Shakespeare's time in an accessible narrative account of the playwright's life.

Shakespeare's Theater

Bentley, G. E. *The Profession of Player in Shakespeare's Time, 1590–1642.* Princeton: Princeton University Press, 1984.

Bentley readably sets forth a wealth of evidence about performance in Shakespeare's time, with special attention to the relations between player and company, and the business of casting, managing, and touring.

Berry, Herbert. *Shakespeare's Playhouses.* New York: AMS Press, 1987.

Berry's six essays collected here discuss (with illustrations) varying aspects of the four playhouses in which Shakespeare had a financial stake: the Theatre in Shoreditch, the Blackfriars, and the first and second Globe.

Berry, Herbert, William Ingram, and Glynne Wickham, eds. *English Professional Theatre, 1530–1660.* Cambridge: Cambridge University Press, 2000.

Wickham presents the government documents designed to control professional players, their plays, and playing places. Ingram handles the professional actors, giving as representative a life of the actor Augustine Phillips, and discussing, among other topics, patrons, acting companies, costumes, props, playbooks, provincial playing, and child actors. Berry treats the twenty-three different London playhouses from 1560 to 1660 for which there are records, including four inns.

Cook, Ann Jennalie. *The Privileged Playgoers of Shakespeare's London.* Princeton: Princeton University Press, 1981.

Cook's work argues, on the basis of sociological, economic, and documentary evidence, that Shakespeare's audience—and the audience for English Renaissance drama generally—consisted mainly of the "privileged."

Greg, W. W. *Dramatic Documents from the Elizabethan Playhouses.* 2 vols. Oxford: Clarendon Press, 1931.

Greg itemizes and briefly describes almost all the play manuscripts that survive from the period 1590 to around 1660, including, among other things, players' parts. His second volume offers facsimiles of selected manuscripts.

Gurr, Andrew. *Playgoing in Shakespeare's London.* Cambridge: Cambridge University Press, 1987.

Gurr charts how the theatrical enterprise developed from its modest beginnings in the late 1560s to become a thriving institution in the 1600s. He argues that there were important changes over the period 1567–1644 in the playhouses, the audience, and the plays.

Harbage, Alfred. *Shakespeare's Audience.* New York: Columbia University Press, 1941.

Harbage investigates the fragmentary surviving evidence to interpret the size, composition, and behavior of Shakespeare's audience.

Hattaway, Michael. *Elizabethan Popular Theatre: Plays in Performance.* London: Routledge & Kegan Paul, 1982.

Beginning with a study of the popular drama of the late Elizabethan age—a description of the stages, performance conditions, and acting of the period—this volume concludes with an analysis of five well-known plays of the 1590s, one of them (*Titus Andronicus*) by Shakespeare.

Shapiro, Michael. *Children of the Revels: The Boy Companies of Shakespeare's Time and Their Plays*. New York: Columbia University Press, 1977.

Shapiro chronicles the history of the amateur and quasi-professional child companies that flourished in London at the end of Elizabeth's reign and the beginning of James's.

The Publication of Shakespeare's Plays

Blayney, Peter W. M. *The First Folio of Shakespeare*. Hanover, Md.: Folger, 1991.

Blayney's accessible account of the printing and later life of the First Folio—an amply illustrated catalogue to a 1991 Folger Shakespeare Library exhibition—analyzes the mechanical production of the First Folio, describing how the Folio was made, by whom and for whom, how much it cost, and its ups and downs (or, rather, downs and ups) since its printing in 1623.

Hinman, Charlton. *The Norton Facsimile: The First Folio of Shakespeare*. 2nd ed. New York: W. W. Norton, 1996.

This facsimile presents a photographic reproduction of an "ideal" copy of the First Folio of Shakespeare; Hinman attempts to represent each page in its most fully corrected state. This second edition includes an important new introduction by Peter W. M. Blayney.

Hinman, Charlton. *The Printing and Proof-Reading of the First Folio of Shakespeare*. 2 vols. Oxford: Clarendon Press, 1963.

In the most arduous study of a single book ever

undertaken, Hinman attempts to reconstruct how the Shakespeare First Folio of 1623 was set into type and run off the press, sheet by sheet. He also provides almost all the known variations in readings from copy to copy.

Key to Famous Lines and Phrases

Fair is foul, and foul is fair . . .   [*Witches*—1.1.12]

So foul and fair a day I have not seen.
    [*Macbeth*—1.3.39]

Nothing in his life
Became him like the leaving it.   [*Malcolm*—1.4.8–9]

Yet do I fear thy nature;
It is too full o' th' milk of human kindness . . .
    [*Lady Macbeth*—1.5.16–17]

Come, you spirits
That tend on mortal thoughts, unsex me here . . .
    [*Lady Macbeth*—1.5.47–48]

Look like th' innocent flower,
But be the serpent under 't.
    [*Lady Macbeth*—1.5.76–78]

If it were done when 'tis done, then 'twere well
It were done quickly.   [*Macbeth*—1.7.1–2]

Is this a dagger which I see before me,
The handle toward my hand?   [*Macbeth*—2.1.44–45]

Sleep that knits up the raveled sleave of care . . .
    [*Macbeth*—2.2.49]

Will all great Neptune's ocean wash this blood
Clean from my hand?   [*Macbeth*—2.2.78–79]

> Naught's had, all's spent,
> Where our desire is got without content.
> [*Lady Macbeth*—3.2.6–7]

We have scorched the snake, not killed it.
[*Macbeth*—3.2.15]

> Duncan is in his grave.
> After life's fitful fever he sleeps well.
> [*Macbeth*—3.2.25–26]

... I am cabined, cribbed, confined, bound in
To saucy doubts and fears.   [*Macbeth*—3.4.26–27]

It will have blood, they say; blood will have blood.
[*Macbeth*—3.4.151]

Double, double toil and trouble;
Fire burn, and cauldron bubble.   [*Witches*—4.1.10–11]

... I'll make assurance double sure ...
[*Macbeth*—4.1.94]

Angels are bright still, though the brightest fell.
[*Malcolm*—4.3.27]

At one fell swoop?   [*Macduff*—4.3.258]

Out, damned spot, out, I say!   [*Lady Macbeth*— 5.1.37]

All the perfumes of Arabia will not sweeten this little hand.   [*Lady Macbeth*—5.1.53–55]

What's done cannot be undone.
[*Lady Macbeth*—5.1.71]

Key to Famous Lines and Phrases

I have lived long enough. My way of life
Is fall'n into the sere, the yellow leaf...
[*Macbeth*—5.3.26–27]

Canst thou not minister to a mind diseased...?
[*Macbeth*—5.3.50]

I have supped full with horrors.   [*Macbeth*—5.5.15]

Tomorrow and tomorrow and tomorrow...
[*Macbeth*—5.5.22]

I 'gin to be aweary of the sun...   [*Macbeth*—5.5.55]

Lay on, Macduff,
And damned be him that first cries "Hold! Enough!"
[*Macbeth*—5.8.38–39]

"JAMES SHAPIRO'S PARTICULAR GIFT AS A LITERARY HISTORIAN IS TO COMBINE GREAT GOOD SENSE WITH DARING IMAGINATIVE REACH."

—Andrew Motion, former poet laureate of the United Kingdom

From the author of *Contested Will*, a thrilling exploration of the chaotic year in which Shakespeare wrote three of his greatest tragedies:

KING LEAR
MACBETH
ANTONY AND CLEOPATRA

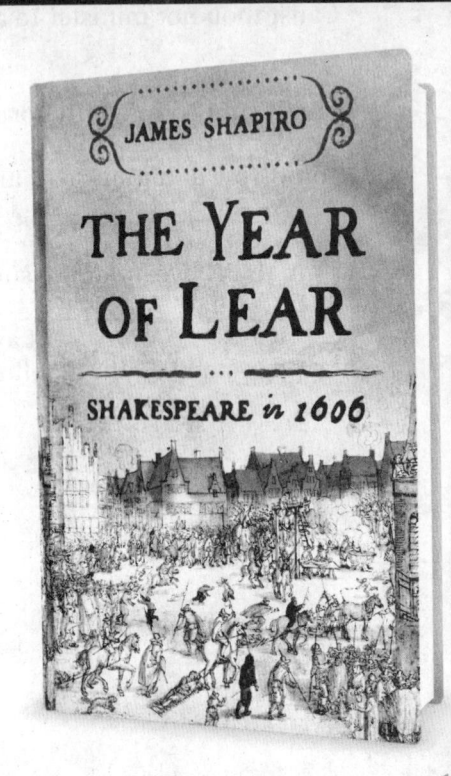

JAMES SHAPIRO
THE YEAR OF LEAR
SHAKESPEARE in 1606

AVAILABLE NOW

SIMON & SCHUSTER
A CBS COMPANY

JAMESSHAPIRO.NET @SIMONBOOKS SIMONANDSCHUSTER.COM